Introduction

Welcome to Learn-a-Language Spanish!

With the aid of these books, students can easily obtain a working knowledge of beginning Spanish. Learning common vocabulary and phrases, then proceeding to verbs and sentence construction gives students the opportunity to learn by themselves with minimum help from adults.

The Spanish language has a consistent spelling and pronunciation pattern. Some marks and accents occur that we don't have in English. The accent mark is a signal that the syllable is to be stressed. All words in Spanish have a "natural" accent that usually occurs in the next to last syllable. The phonetic guide that accompanies many of the words in Spanish will help in both pronunciation and in accenting the proper syllables. The stressed syllable will appear in **bold** type.

The following pronunciation guide will help with Spanish sounds.

Vowels	How to Pronounce	English Sample
a	ah	Open wide and say "ah."
e	eh	egg
i	ee	see
o	oh	only
u	oo	boot

Consonants

The consonants are pronounced much like those in English with the following exceptions:

h	always silent	
j	h	hat
qu	k	kite
ll (double l)	y	yet

This series includes words, phrases, sentences, puzzles, games, and an easy-reference vocabulary list.

Becoming fluent in any language requires practice. Encourage students to name obj⸻ ⸻ and at school in Spanish and to try their new skill with Spanish-speaking peo⸻

Occupations/Las Ocupaciones

*(oh-koo-pah-**syohn**-ehs)*

Read the word. Say it aloud. Write the word and say it again as you write it.

el doctor
*(dohk-**tohr**)* _____

la piloto
*(pee-**loh**-toh)* _____

la abogada
*(ah-boh-**gah**-doh)* _____

el bombero
*(bohm-**beh**-roh)* _____

el/la dentista
*(den-**tees**-tah)* _____

le policía
*(poh-lee-**see**-yah)* _____

el ingeniero
*(een-heh-nee-**eh**-roh)* _____

el músico
*(**moo**-see-koh)* _____

el cartero
*(kar-**teh**-roh)* _____

el plomero
*(ploh-**meh**-roh)* _____

FS-23102 Spanish—Elementary Level 2

Occupations/Las Ocupaciones

el jardinero
*(har-dee-**neh**-roh)* _____

el farmacéutico
*(fahr-mah-**seh**-oo-tee-koh)* _____

el panadero
*(pah-nah-**deh**-roh)* _____

_____

el banquero
*(bahn-**keh**-roh)* _____

el cocinero
*(koh-see-**neh**-roh)* _____

el peluquero
*(peh-loo-**keh**-roh)* _____

el veterinario
*(veh-teh-ree-**nah**-ree-yoh)* _____

la bibliotecario
*(bee-bleeoh-teh-**kah**-ree-yoh)* _____

_____

el lechero
*(leh-**cheh**-roh)* _____

la secretaria
*(seh-kreh-**tah**-ree-yah)* _____

el joyero
*(ho-**yeh**-roh)* _____

Occupations/Las Ocupaciones

Finish the following sentences. Write the correct occupation on each line in English (inglés) and in Spanish (español).

	English/inglés	Spanish/español
After the plane landed, I got to meet the	_____	_____
Cindy had a toothache. She went to the	_____	_____
Joe had the mumps. He went to the	_____	_____
Becky's sink broke. She called a	_____	_____
The bridge was built by an	_____	_____
We gave our mail to the	_____	_____
Dan loves the guitar. He wants to be a	_____	_____
My dad likes to make pastries. That's why he became a	_____	_____
Ralph likes to put out fires. He is a	_____	_____
Marc gave me a great haircut. He is a wonderful	_____	_____

FS-23102 Spanish—Elementary Level 2

Places in the Community/Lugares en la Comunidad

*(loo-**gah**-rehs en lah koh-moo-**nee**-dahd)*

Read the word. Say it aloud. Write the word and say it again as you write it.

el restaurante
*(ehl rehs-tah-oo-**rhan**-teh)* _____

el parque
*(ehl **pahr**-keh)* _____

el hospital
*(ehl ohs-pee-t**ahl**)* _____

la iglesia
*(lah ee-**glehs**-ee-yah)* _____

el cine
*(ehl **see**-neh)* _____

la biblioteca
*(lah bee-blee-oh-**teh**-kah)* _____

el teatro
*(ehl teh-**ah**-troh)* _____

el hotel
*(ehl oh-**tehl**)* _____

el museo
*(ehl moo-**seh**-oh)* _____

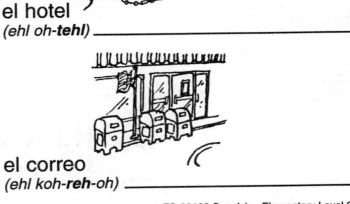

el correo
*(ehl koh-**reh**-oh)* _____

el banco
*(ehl **bahn**-koh)* _____

la panadería
*(lah pah-nah-deh-**ree**-yah)* _____

_____

la farmacia
*(lah fahr-**mah**-see-yah)* _____

la carnicería
*(lah kahr-nee-seh-**ree**-yah)* _____

_____

la zapatería
*(lah sah-pah-teh-**ree**-yah)* _____

el salón de belleza
*(ehl sah-**lohn** deh beh-**yeh**-sah)* _____

_____

el supermercado
*(ehl soo-pehr-mehr-**kah**-doh)* _____

la peluquería
*(lah peh-loo-keh-**ree**-yah)* _____

_____

el zoológico
*(ehl soh-**loh**-hee-koh)* _____

la tienda
*(lah tee-**ehn**-dah)* _____

la estación de bomberos
*(lah ehs-tah-**syohn** _____
deh bohm-**beh**-rohs)*

_____

Nombre _____

Occupations and Places/Ocupaciones y Lugares

Write each occupation to match the work places.

Ocupaciones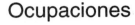

1. el hospital _____

2. la biblioteca _____

3. el correo _____

4. la farmacia _____

5. el zoológico _____

6. el salón de belleza _____

7. el teatro _____

8. el restaurante _____

9. el banco _____

10. la estación de bomberos _____

11. la panadería _____

The Community/La Comunidad

*(lah koh-moo-**nee**-dahd)*

Find and circle the Spanish words hidden in the puzzle. Translate the words into English.

E	O	F	A	R	M	A	C	I	A	H	O
P	T	C	E	U	Q	R	A	P	O	D	Z
A	I	N	N	M	V	E	G	T	A	T	O
N	G	A	A	A	G	O	E	C	U	O	O
A	L	M	X	R	B	L	R	B	D	E	L
D	E	M	K	A	U	E	Z	E	A	R	O
E	S	U	X	I	M	A	O	V	P	R	G
R	I	D	E	R	K	Z	T	E	U	O	I
I	A	N	E	F	V	C	I	S	S	C	C
A	I	P	T	I	E	N	D	A	E	U	O
C	U	B	T	E	A	T	R	O	E	R	M
S	J	A	C	E	T	O	I	L	B	I	B

Spanish/español

1. BANCO
2. BIBLIOTECA
3. CINE
4. CORREO
5. TEATRO
6. FARMACIA
7. HOTEL
8. IGLESIA
9. MUSEO
10. PANADERÍA
11. PARQUE
12. RESTAURANTE
13. SUPERMERCADO
14. TIENDA
15. ZOOLOGICO

English/inglés

1. _____
2. _____
3. _____
4. _____
5. _____
6. _____
7. _____
8. _____
9. _____
10. _____
11. _____
12. _____
13. _____
14. _____
15. _____

Occupations and Community Review
Repaso de Ocupaciones y Comunidad

Write, in Spanish, the places in the community that go with the occupations listed.

Occupation Ocupacion	Places in the Community Lugares en la comunidad
1. peluquero	_____
2. banquero	_____
3. cocinero	_____
4. farmacéutico	_____
5. jardinero	_____
6. cartero	_____
7. músico	_____
8. doctor	_____
9. bibliotecario	_____
10. veterinario	_____

Transportation/Transporte
(trahns-**pohr**-teh)

Read the word. Say it aloud. Write the word and say it again as you write it.

el carro
*(ehl **kah**-roh)* _____

el barco
*(ehl **bahr**-koh)* _____

el autobús
*(ehl ah-toh-**boos**)* _____

la bicicleta
*(lah bee-see-**kleh**-tah)* _____

el avión
*(ehl ah-**vyohn**)* _____

la motocicleta
*(lah moh-toh-see-**kleh**-tah)* _____

el tren
(ehl trehn) _____

el helicóptero
*(ehl eh-lee-**kohp**-teh-roh)* _____

el camión
*(ehl kah-**myohn**)* _____

los patines
*(lohs pah-**tee**-nehs)* _____

Transportation/Transporte

la patineta
*(lah pah-tee-**neh**-tah)* _____

la carreta
*(lah kah-**reh**-tah)* _____

el patinete
*(ehl pah-tee-**neh**-teh)* _____

el submarino
*(ehl soob-mah-**ree**-noh)* _____

el barco de vela
*(ehl **bahr**-koh deh **veh**-lah)* _____

_____

la limosina
*(lah lee-moh-**see**-nah)* _____

el taxi
*(ehl **tahk**-see)* _____

la nave
*(lah **nah**-veh)* _____

la nave espacial
*(lah **nah**-veh ehs-pah-**seeyal**)* _____

_____

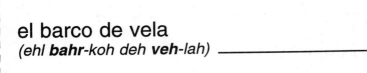

_____

Vehicles/Vehículos

*(vee-**hee**-koo-lohs)*

Use the clues to help you name each vehicle. Write the words in English and in Spanish on the lines. Don't forget to include **el** or **la**.

Clues Pistas *(**peece**-tahs)*	English word Palabra en inglés	Spanish word Palabra en español
two wings, flies	_____	_____
two wheels, handlebars	_____	_____
four wheels, big	_____	_____
floats, ocean, lake, small	_____	_____
four wheels, family transportation	_____	_____
two wheels, motor	_____	_____
six wheels, passengers, fare	_____	_____
flies, propeller	_____	_____
many wheels, track	_____	_____
eight wheels, pair	_____	_____

FS-23102 Spanish—Elementary Level 2

Transportation Everywhere
Transporte en Todas Partes
*(trahns-**pohr**-teh ehn **toh**-dahs **pahr**-tes)*

Write the correct Spanish words for the kinds of transportation that can be used in each place.

(ocean)

_____   _____

_____   _____

(land)

_____   _____

_____   _____

_____   _____

_____   _____

(air)

_____   _____   _____

Holidays and Celebrations
Días Festivos y Celebraciones
*(dee-ahs fehs-**tee**-vohs ee seh-leh-brah-**syohn**-ehs)*

Read each phrase. Say it aloud. Write the phrase and say it again as you write it.

el Año Nuevo
(New Year)
*(ehl **ah**-nyoh **nueh**-voh)* _____

_____

la Pascua
(Easter)
*(lah **pahs**-kwah)* _____

_____

el Día de San Valentín
(Valentine's Day)
*(ehl **dee**-ah deh sahn* _____
*vah-lehn-**teen**)*

_____

el Día de las Madres
(Mother's Day)
*(ehl **dee**-ah deh lahs* _____
***mah**-drehs)*

_____

el Día de San Patricio
(Saint Patrick's Day)
*(ehl **dee**-ah deh sahn* _____
*pah-**tree**-syoh*

_____

el Día de los Padres
(Father's Day)
*(ehl **dee**-ah deh lohs* _____
***pah**-drehs)*

_____

     FS-23102 Spanish—Elementary Level 2

Nombre _____

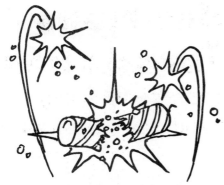

el Día de la Independencia
(Independence Day)
*(ehl **dee**-ah deh lah* _____
*een-deh-pehn-**dehn**-see-ah)*

_____

la Navidad
(Christmas)
*(lah nah-vee-**dahd**)* _____

_____

el Día de Acción de Gracias
(Thanksgiving Day)
*(ehl **dee**-ah deh ahk-see-**ohn** _____
*deh **grah**-see-ahs)*

_____

el cumpleaños
(birthday)
*(ehl koom-pleh-**ah**-nyohs)* _____

_____

la Nochebuena
(Christmas Eve)
*(lah noh-cheh-**bweh**-nah)* _____

_____

Holiday Time/Días de Fiesta
(fyehs-tah)

Label the pictures with the correct Spanish words to name each holiday.

_____

_____

_____

_____

_____

_____

_____

_____

_____

_____

FS-23102 Spanish—Elementary Level 2

Greetings/Saludos
(sah-**loo**-dohs)

Read each word or phrase. Say it aloud. Write the word or phrase and say it again as you write it.

hello   hola
                             (**oh**-lah)   _____

goodbye   adiós
                             (ah-dee-**ohs**)   _____

How are you?   ¿Cómo está usted?
                             (**koh**-moh es-**tah** oos-**tehd**) _____

Fine, thank you.   Bien, gracias.
                             (bee-**yehn grah**-see-yahs) _____

Good morning.   Buenos días.
                             (**bweh**-nohs **dee**-ahs)   _____

Good afternoon.   Buenas tardes.
                             (**bweh**-nahs **tahr**-dehs) _____

Good evening.   Buenas noches.
                             (**bweh**-nahs **noh**-chehs) _____

yes   sí
                             (see)   _____

no   no
                             (noh)   _____

Thank you.   Gracias.
                             (**grah**-see-yahs)   _____

You're welcome.   De nada.
                             (deh **nah**-dah)   _____

Common Phrases/Frases Comunes

(koh-**moo**-nehs)

Read each word or phrase. Say it aloud. Write the phrase or word and say it again as you write it.

What is your name?	¿Cómo se llama? (**koh**-moh seh **yah**-mah)	_____
My name is...	Me llamo... (meh **yah**-moh)	_____
How old are you?	¿Cuántos años tiene? (**kwahn**-tohs **ahn**-yohs **tyeh**-neh)	_____
I am ___ years old.	Tengo ___ años. (**tehn**-goh ___ **ahn**-yohs)	_____
Do you want to play?	¿Quiere jugar? (kee-**eh**-reh **hoo**-ghar)	_____
Where do you live?	¿Dónde vive? (**dohn**-deh **vee**-veh)	_____
Who?	¿Quién? (kyehn)	_____
What?	¿Qué? (keh)	_____
When?	¿Cuándo? (**kwahn**-doh)	_____
Where?	¿Dónde? (**dohn**-deh)	_____
Why?	¿Por qué? (pohr **keh**)	_____
How?	¿Cómo? (**koh**-moh)	_____
Where is...	¿Dónde está...? (**dohn**-deh ehs-**tah**)	_____
How many...	¿Cuántos? (**kwahn**-tohs)	_____

FS-23102 Spanish—Elementary Level 2

Nombre _____

Restaurant or Store?/Restaurante o Tienda
(rehs-tah-oo-**rahn**-teh oh tee-**ehn**-dah)

Read each word or phrase. Say the word or phrase aloud.
Write the word or phrase and say it again as you write it.

May I have the menu?   ¿Me da el menú?
                         *(meh dah ehl meh-**noo**)*   _____

I would like...   Me gustaría...
                         *(meh goos-tah-**ree**-ah)*   _____

Do you have...?   ¿Tiene...?
                         *(**tyeh**-neh)*   _____

May I have the bill?   ¿Me da la cuenta?
                         *(meh dah lah **kwen**-tah)*   _____

Where...?   ¿Dónde?
                         *(**dohn**-deh)*   _____

How much does it cost?   ¿Cuánto cuesta?
                         *(**kwan**-toh **kwehs**-tah)* _____

I will take it.   Me lo llevo.
                         *(meh loh **yeh**-voh)*   _____

I am just looking.   Sólo estoy mirando.
                         *(**soh**-loh **ehs**-toy mee-**rahn**-doh)* _____

Can you help me?   ¿Me puede ayudar?
                         *(meh **pweh**-deh ah-yoo-**dahr**)* _____

Where is the restroom?   ¿Dónde está el baño?
                         *(**dohn**-deh ehs-**tah** ehl **bah**-nyoh)* _____

Women   Damas
                         *(**dah**-mahs)*   _____

Men   Caballeros/Hombres
                         *(kah-bah-**yeh**-rohs)/(**ohm**-brehs)* _____

Where is the telephone? ¿Dónde está el teléfono?
                         *(**dohn**-deh ehs-**tah** ehl teh-**leh**-foh-noh)*

19

Nombre ______________________________

A New Friend/Un Amigo Nuevo

*(oon ah-**mee**-go **nueh**-voh)*

Write the following conversation in Spanish:

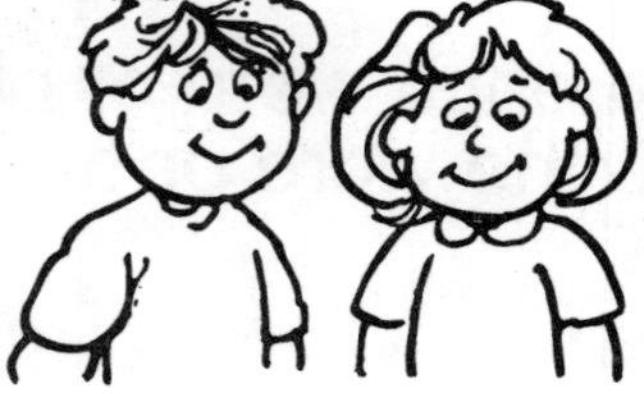

Susan: Good morning, Mark.

____

Mark: Hello, Susan. How are you?

____

Susan: Fine, thank you.

____

Mark: How old are you?

____

Susan: I am ten years old.

____

Mark: Do you want to play?

____

Susan: Yes. Thank you.

____

Nombre _____

Hidden Words/Palabras Escondidas

*(pah-**lah**-brahs ehs-kohn-**dee**-dahs)*

Find and circle the Spanish words hidden in the puzzle. Write each word in English.

H	H	S	D	O	N	D	E	O
C	O	O	I	G	I	G	N	E
U	N	L	M	F	I	S	P	K
A	E	X	A	B	A	R	Z	S
N	I	G	A	I	R	Ú	V	O
D	U	F	C	O	N	E	D	I
O	Q	A	M	E	K	Q	S	D
A	R	O	M	X	D	M	U	A
G	C	B	S	A	M	A	D	E

ADIOS   HOMBRES
COMO   MENÚ
CUANDO   NO
DAMAS   QUE
DONDE   QUIEN
GRACIAS   SI
HOLA

Spanish	English	Spanish	English
1. ADIÓS _____		8. HOMBRES_____	
2. CÓMO _____		9. MENÚ _____	
3. CUÁNDO _____		10. NO _____	
4. DAMAS _____		11. QUÉ_____	
5. DÓNDE _____		12. QUIÉN _____	
6. GRACIAS_____		13. SÍ _____	
7. HOLA_____			

Time/Hora

(*oh*-rah)

Read each word or phrase. Say it aloud.

What time it it?	¿Qué hora es? (*keh* **oh**-*rah ehs*)	
It is ...	Es la... (*ehs lah*)	-used if the hour is one
	Son las... (*sohn lahs*)	-used if the hour is two or more
...one o'clock	...una (**oo**-*nah*)	other hours are same as the numbers
...two fifteen	...dos y quince. (*dohs ee* **keen**-*seh*)	
...three thirty	...tres y media. (*trehs ee* **meh**-*dyah*)	
...quarter to six	...cuarto para las seis. (**kwar**-*toh* **pah**-*rah lahs* **seh**-*ees*)	
	or ...siete menos quince. (**syeh**-*teh* **meh**-*nohs* **keen**-*seh*)	
...in the morning.	...de la mañana. (*deh lah mah*-**nyah**-*nah*)	
...in the afternoon.	...de la tarde. (*deh lah* **tar**-*deh*)	
...in the evening	...de la noche. (*deh lah* **noh**-*cheh*)	
midnight	medianoche (*meh-deyah*-**noh**-*cheh*)	
midday	mediodía (*meh-deyoh*-**dee**-*ah*)	

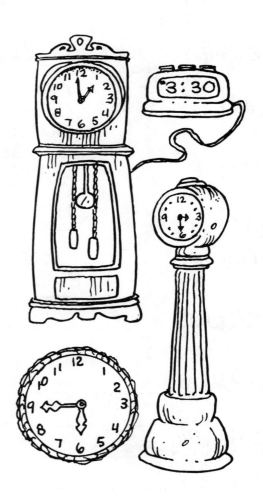

Do You Have the Time?
¿Tienes la Hora?

Answer the questions in Spanish. Say the words as you write them.

¿Qué hora es?	Son las...
9:20 a.m.	_____
11:15 p.m.	_____
12:00 a.m.	_____
12:00 p.m.	_____
7:45 a.m.	_____
5:20 p.m.	_____
3:17 p.m.	_____

	Es la...
1:30 p.m.	_____
1:30 a.m.	_____
1: 10 a.m.	_____

At What Time?/¿A Qué Hora?

*(ah-keh-**oh**-rah)*

Answer the questions below in Spanish. Remember to write morning, afternoon, or night.

What time do you get up in the morning?

_____

What time do you have breakfast?

_____

What time do you go to school or work?

_____

What time do you have lunch?

_____

What time do you get home?

_____

What time do you eat dinner?

_____

What time do you go to bed?

_____

Nombre _____

Prepositional Phrases/Frases Preposicionales

*(preh-poh-see-see-oh-**nah**-lehs)*

A preposition is a word that shows direction, such as **in, on, behind**, and **over**. Read each word or phrase. Write the word or phrase and say it again as you write it.

sobre/encima de *(**soh**-breh)/(ehn-**see**-mah deh)*	above	_____
detrás de *(deh-**trahs** deh)*	behind	_____
debajo de *(deh-**bah**-hoh deh)*	below	_____
bajo *(**bah**-hoh)*	beneath	_____
entre *(**ehn**-treh)*	between	_____
en *(ehn)*	in	_____
dentro de *(**dehn**-troh deh)*	inside	_____
detrás de *(deh-**trahs** deh)*	in back	_____
delante de *(deh-**lahn**-teh deh)*	in front	_____
en *(ehn)*	on	_____
fuera de *(**fweh**-rah deh)*	outside of	_____
sobre/por encima de *(**soh**-breh)/(pohr ehn-**see**-mah deh)*	over	_____
debajo de *deh-**bah**-hoh deh)*	under	_____

Nombre _____

Preposition Practice/Práctica de Preposiciones

*(preh-poh-see-see-**oh**-nehs)*

Read the phrase in Spanish. Each one is called a **prepositional phrase**. Say it aloud. Match the phrase to the picture by drawing lines between the pairs.

debajo de

encima de

delante de

bajo

dentro de

en

fuera de

detrás de

entre

Writing Prepositions/Escribiendo las Preposiciones
*(ehs-kree-**byehn**-doh)*

Look at each picture. Write the correct preposition in Spanish.

_____   _____

_____   _____

_____   _____

_____   _____

_____   _____

Personal Pronouns/Pronombres Personales

*(proh-**nohm**-brehs pehr-soh-**nah**-lehs)*

Read each word. Say it aloud. Write it and say it again as you write it. Personal pronouns: I, you, she, he, we, you (plural). There are two forms of the pronoun "you" in Spanish. The familiar "tú" is used when talking to children, friends, and family. The formal "usted" is used at all other times.

I	yo *(yoh)*	_____
you, familiar	tú *(too)*	_____
you, formal	usted *(oos-**tehd**)*	_____
she	ella *(**eh**-yah)*	_____
he	él *(ehl)*	_____
we	nosotros *(noh-**soh**-trohs)*	_____
you, plural	ustedes *(oos-**teh**-dehs)*	_____
they, feminine	ellas *(**eh**-yahs)*	_____
they, masculine	ellos *(**eh**-yohs)*	_____

Pronoun Matching/Emparajando los Pronombres
*(ehm-pah-rah-**hahn**-doh lohs proh-**nohm**-brehs)*

Draw a line between each matching pair of pronouns in English and Spanish.

we	ellos
you, plural	usted
I	él
she	ustedes
they, feminine	nosotros
you, formal	ella
he	yo
they, masculine	tú
you, familiar	ellas

Present Tense Verbs/Verbos en el Presente
(*vehr*-bohs ehn ehl preh-**sehn**-teh)

to be/estar
(ehs-**tahr**)

Read each sentence. Say it aloud. Write it in Spanish and say it again as you write it.

Yo estoy en la casa.
*(yoh ehs-**toy** ehn
lah **kah**-sah)*

I am in the house.

_____

Tú estás en la casa.
*(too ehs-**tahs** ehn
lah **kah**-sah)*

You (one person, friend
or relative) are in the house. _____

Usted está en la casa.
*(oos-**tehd** ehs-**tah** ehn
lah **kah**-sah)*

You (formal, one person)
are in the house.

_____

Él está en la casa.
*(ehl ehs-**tah** ehn
lah **kah**-sah)*

He is in the house.

_____

Ella está en la casa.
*(**eh**-yah ehs-**tah** ehn
lah **kah**-sah)*

She is in the house.

_____

Nosotros estamos
en la casa.
*(noh-**soh**-trohs ehs-**tah**-mohs
ehn lah **kah**-sah)*

We are in the house.

_____

Ustedes están
en la casa.
*(oos-**teh**-dehs ehs-**tahn**
ehn lah **kah**-sah)*

You (more than one
person) are in the house.

_____

Ellos están en la casa.
*(**eh**-yohs ehs-**tahn** ehn
lah **kah**-sah)*

They (males) are
in the house.

_____

Ellas están en la casa.
*(**eh**-yahs ehs-**tahn** ehn
lah **kah**-sah)*

They (females) are
in the house.

_____

Using the Verb *To Be*/Usando el Verbo *Estar*

(oo-sahn-doh ehl vehr-boh)

Read the sentences. Say them aloud.
Draw a picture to go with each sentence.

Usted está en la casa.

Nosotros estamos en la casa.

Tú estás en la casa.

Yo estoy en la casa.

Ella está en la casa.

Ellos están en la casa.

Él está en la casa.

Ustedes están en la casa.

Ellas están en la casa.

Practicing the Verb *To Be*
Practicando el Verbo *Estar*

Write the correct Spanish word to complete each sentence.
The first one is done for you. Write each sentence in English.

Él ___está___ en la casa.   He is in the house.

Nosotros _____ en la casa.   _____

Yo _____ en la casa.   _____

Ustedes _____ en la casa.   _____

Ellas _____ en la casa.   _____

Ella _____ en la casa.   _____

Usted _____ en la casa.   _____

Tú _____ en la casa.   _____

Ellos _____ en la casa.   _____

Feelings and Emotions
Los Estados Físicos y Emocionales
*(lohs ehs-**tah**-dohs **fee**-see-kohs ee eh-moh-syon-**ahl**-ehs)*
Read each word. Say it aloud. Write the word and say it again as you write it.

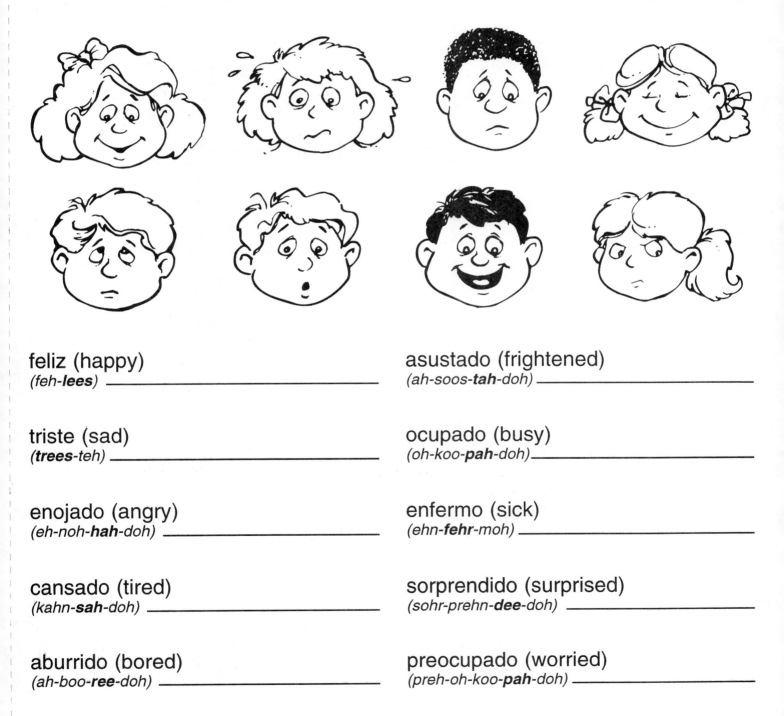

feliz (happy)
*(feh-**lees**)* _____

triste (sad)
*(**trees**-teh)* _____

enojado (angry)
*(eh-noh-**hah**-doh)* _____

cansado (tired)
*(kahn-**sah**-doh)* _____

aburrido (bored)
*(ah-boo-**ree**-doh)* _____

asustado (frightened)
*(ah-soos-**tah**-doh)* _____

ocupado (busy)
*(oh-koo-**pah**-doh)* _____

enfermo (sick)
*(ehn-**fehr**-moh)* _____

sorprendido (surprised)
*(sohr-prehn-**dee**-doh)* _____

preocupado (worried)
*(preh-oh-koo-**pah**-doh)* _____

How Do You Feel?/¿Como Se Siente?

*(**koh**-meh seh see-**ehn**-teh)*

Read each sentence. Say it aloud. Write it and say it again as you write it.
Translate each sentence into English. The first one is done for you.

El niño está cansado.
*(ehl **nee**-nyoh ehs-**tah**
kahn-**sah**-doh)*

_____ El niño está cansado. _____

_____ The boy is tired. _____

La niña está cansada.
*(lah **nee**-nyah ehs-**tah**
kahn-**sah**-dah)*

_____

_____

Yo estoy feliz.
*(yoh ehs-t**oee** feh-**lees**)*

_____

_____

Ellos están enojados.
*(**eh**-yohs ehs-**tahn**
eh-noh-**hah**-dohs)*

_____

_____

Ellas están enojados.
*(**eh**-yahs ehs-**tahn**
eh-noh-**hah**-dahs)*

_____

_____

Nosotros estamos tristes.
*(nohs-**oh**-trohs ehs-**tah**-mohs
trees-tehs)*

_____

_____

Tú estás enfermo.
*(**too** ehs-**tahs** ehn-**fehr**-moh)*

_____

_____

Ustedes están
preocupados.
*(oos-**teh**-dehs ehs-**tahn**
preh-oh-koo-**pah**-dohs)*

_____

_____

Usted está ocupado.
*(oos-**tehd** ehs-**tah**
oh-koo-**pah**-doh)*

_____

_____

Writing About Feelings
Escribiendo Sobre los Sentimientos
(**soh**-breh sehn-tee-**myehn**-tohs)

Write the missing Spanish words.

El niño _____ cansado.
_is_

La mamá está _____ .
happy

_____ estamos ocupados.
_We_

Las niñas _____ tristes.
are

_____ estoy sorprendido.
_I_

Ustedes _____ enojados.
are

La niña está _____ .
scared

Yo estoy _____ .
surprised

Nosotros _____ enfermos.
are

Tú _____ preocupado.
are

_____ estás preocupada.
You

The Verb To Play/El Verbo Jugar

(hoo-**gahr**)

Read each sentence. Say it aloud. Write it and say it again as you write it.

Yo **juego** en el parque.
*(yoh **hweh**-goh ehn ehl **pahr**-keh)*

I play in the park.

_____

Tú **juegas** en el parque.
*(too **hweh**-gahs ehn ehl **pahr**-keh)*

You play in the park.

_____

Usted **juega** en el parque.
*(oos-tehd **hweh**-gah ehn ehl **pahr**-que)*

You play in the park.

_____

Él **juega** en el parque.
*(ehl **hweh**-gah ehn ehl **pahr**-keh)*

He plays in the park.

_____

Ella **juega** en el parque.
*(**eh**-yah **hweh**-gah ehn ehl **pahr**-keh)*

She plays in the park.

_____

Nosotros **jugamos** en el parque.
*(noh-**soh**-trohs hoo-**gah**-mohs ehn ehl **pahr**-keh)*

We play in the park.

_____

Ustedes **juegan** en el parque.
*(oos-**teh**-dehs **hweh**-gahn ehn ehl **pahr**-keh)*

You play in the park.

_____

Ellos **juegan** en el parque.
*(**eh**-yohs **hweh**-gahn ehn ehl **pahr**-keh)*

They play in the park.

_____

Ellas **juegan** en el parque.
*(**eh**-yahs **hweh**-gahn ehn ehl **pahr**-keh)*

They play in the park.

_____

Using the Verb *To Play*/Usando el Verbo *Jugar*

Look at the pictures. Write a sentence in Spanish using the verb **jugar** to show what is happening in each picture.

_____

_____

_____

_____

Pronouns and the Verb *To Play*
Pronombres y El Verbo *Jugar*

Write the correct form of **jugar** to complete each sentence. The first one is done for you.

Yo _____juego_____ en el parque.

Ella _____ en el parque.

Nosotros _____ en el parque.

Usted _____ en el parque.

Ellos _____ en el parque.

Ellas _____ en el parque.

Ustedes _____ en el parque.

Tú _____ en el parque.

Él _____ en el parque.

The Verb *To Go*/El Verbo *Ir*

(eer)

Read each sentence. Say it aloud. Write it and say it again as you write it. Write it in English. **Al** means **to the** before masculine nouns. **A la** means **to the** before feminine nouns.

Yo voy a la biblioteca.
*(yoh voy ah lah bee-blee-oh-**teh**-kah)*

_____   I go to the library.

Tú vas a la iglesia.
*(too vahs ah la ee-**gleh**-seeyah)*

_____   _____

Usted va al parque.
*(oos-**tehd** vah ahl **pahr**-keh)*

_____   _____

Él va al restaurante.
*(ehl vah ahl rehs-tah-oo-**rahn**-teh)*

_____   _____

Ella va al cine.
*(eh-yah vah ahl **see**-neh)*

_____   _____

Nosotros vamos
a la tienda.
*(noh-**soh**-trohs **vah**-mohs ah lah **tee**-yehn-dah)*

_____   _____

Ustedes van
a la panadería.
*(oos-**teh**-dehs vahn ah lah pah-nah-deh-**ree**-yah*

_____   _____

Ellos van al banco.
*(**eh**-yohs vahn ahl **bahn**-koh)*

_____   _____

Ellas van
al supermercado.
*(**eh**-yahs vahn ahl soo-pehr-mehr-**kah**-doh)*

_____   _____

Using the Verb *To Go*
Usando el Verbo *Ir*

Write Spanish sentences on the lines to show the correct order in which the girls are going to each place. Use the verb **ir (to go)**.

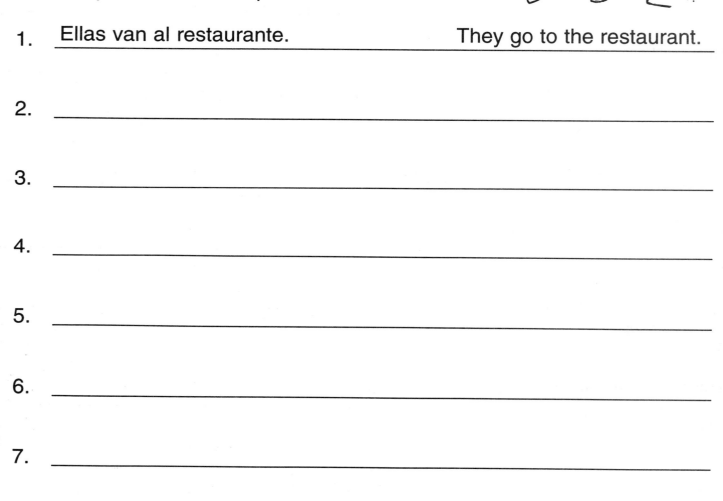

1-restaurant   5-store
2-bank   6-movie theater
3- park   7-library
4-bakery   8-supermarket

1. Ellas van al restaurante.   They go to the restaurant.

2. _____

3. _____

4. _____

5. _____

6. _____

7. _____

8. _____

The Verb *To See*/El Verbo Ver

(vehr)

Read each sentence. Say it aloud. Write the sentence and say it again as you write it. Write it in English. The first one is done for you.

Yo veo la estrella.
*(yoh **veh**-oh lah ehs-**treh**-yah)*   _____   I see the star.

Tú ves la estrella.
*(too vehs lah ehs-**treh**-yah)*   _____   _____

Él ve la estrella.
*(ehl veh lah ehs-**treh**-yah)*   _____   _____

Ella ve la estrella.
*(**eh**-yah veh
lah ehs-**treh**-yah)*   _____   _____

Nosotros vemos la
estrella.
*(noh-**soh**-trohs **veh**-mohs
lah ehs-**treh**-yah)*   _____   _____

Ustedes ven la estrella.
*(oo-**steh**-dehs vehn
lah ehs-**treh**-yah)*   _____   _____

Ellos ven la estrella.
*(**eh**-yohs vehn
lah ehs-**treh**-yah)*   _____   _____

Ellas ven la estrella.
*(**eh**-yahs vehn
lah ehs-**treh**-yah)*   _____   _____

Using the Verb *To See*
Usando el Verbo Ver

Write the missing verb (ver) in the sentence. Read it aloud.

Yo _____ el carro.

Ella _____ la niña.

Nosotros _____ los círculos.

Los niños _____ los plátanos.

Tú _____ tres camisas.

Él _____ el jardín.

Las tías _____ las sillas.

Yo _____ el vestido morado.

FS-23102 Spanish—Elementary Level 2

The Verb *To Have*/El Verbo *Tener*

(teh-nehr)

Read each sentence. Say it aloud. Write the sentence and say it again as you write it. Write it in English. The first one is done for you.

Yo tengo la manzana.
(yoh tehn-goh
lah mahn-sah-nah)

_____   I have the apple.

Tú tienes la manzana.
(too tee-eh-nehs
lah mahn-sah-nah)

_____   _____

Él tiene la manzana.
(ehl tee-eh-neh
lah mahn-sah-nah)

_____   _____

Ella tiene la manzana.
(eh-yah tee-eh-neh
lah mahn-sah-nah)

_____   _____

Nosotros tenemos
la manzana.
(noh-soh-trohs tehn-eh-mohs
lah mahn-sah-nah)

_____   _____

Ustedes tienen
la manzana.
(oo-steh-dehs tee-eh-nehn
lah mahn-sah-nah)

_____   _____

Ellos tienen la manzana.
(eh-yohs tee-eh-nehn
lah mahn-sah-nah)

_____   _____

Ellas tienen la manzana.
(eh-yahs tee-eh-nehn
lah mahn-sah-nah)

_____   _____

Using the Verb *To Have*
Usando el Verbo *Tener*

Write the correct form of the verb (tener) in the line to complete each sentence. Read the sentence aloud. Write it in English. The first one is done for you.

1. Yo _____ una maestra.   _____ I have a teacher.

2. Él _____ dos lápices azules.   _____

3. Fred _____ un carro rojo.   _____

4. Ana _____ tres naranjas.   _____

5. Veronica y Daniela _____   _____
   un barco.

6. José y Victor _____ un   _____
   camión verde.

7. Tú _____ diez años.   _____

8. Ustedes _____ uvas.   _____

Verb Practice
Práctica con los Verbos

Read each English sentence. Fill in the blanks with
the correct Spanish words. Read each sentence aloud.

1. I see the house.   Yo _____ la _____.

2. He plays in the garden.   Él _____ en el _____.

3. Mom goes to the store.   Mamá _____ a la _____.

4. Dad is in the museum.   Papá _____ en el _____.

5. Cindy plays with Sam.   Cindy _____ con Sam.

6. She sees the classroom.   Ella _____ el _____.

7. Frank goes to the library. Frank _____ a la _____.

8. The girl is in the bank.   La niña _____ en el _____.

9. Mom and Dad go to   Mamá y papá _____ al _____.
   the movies.

10. We see the school. Nosotros _____ la _____.

Write each sentence in Spanish. Say it as you write it.

1. I see an apple. _____.

2. Mom goes to the market. _____.

3. Bob is in the restaurant. _____.

Nombre _____

Common Phrases Review
Repaso de Frases Comunes

Write a conversation for the following scene:

You have just met your friend for lunch at a restaurant. Greet him/her and ask the waiter for a menu. Order your meal and make sure you include a protein, a vegetable, a fruit, and a beverage. Ask for the bill, and say good-bye to your friend.

_____

_____

_____

_____

_____

_____

_____

_____

Prepositional Phrases Review
Repaso de Frases Preposicionales

Read the English sentences and write the Spanish words that are missing.
The first one is done for you.

The vase is on the table.　　　　El vaso está ____en____ la mesa.

Dad is behind mom.　　　　El papá está _____ la mamá.

Dad is in front of Grandma.　　　　El papá está _____ la abuela.

The lollipop is in my mouth.　　　　La paleta está _____ mi boca.

Uncle is between the girls.　　　　El tío está _____ las niñas.

The girl is outside the house.　　　　La niña está _____ la casa.

Grandpa is inside the house.　　　　El abuelo está _____ la casa.

The jacket is over the shirt.　　　　La chaqueta está _____
la camisa.

The restaurant is above the
library.　　　　El restaurante está _____
la biblioteca.

The book is under the desk.　　　　El libro está _____
el escritorio.

The paper is under the hand.　　　　El papel está _____
la mano.

Nombre _____

Prepositions Crossword Puzzle
Crucigrama de Preposiciones

Write the words in Spanish in the spaces.

Across
1. over
2. inside
3. in back
4. outside of

Down
5. below
6. above
7. in front
8. behind
9. in
10. beneath
11. between

FS-23102 Spanish—Elementary Level 2

Ordinal Numbers First to Tenth
Numeros Ordinales Primero a Décimo
*(ohr-dee-**nah**-lehs)*

Read the words. Say them aloud. Write the words and say them again as you write them.

primero (first)
*(pree-**meh**-ro)*
_____

segundo
*(seh-**goon**-do)*
_____

tercero
*(tehr-**seh**-ro)*
_____

cuarto
*(**kwahr**-to)*
_____

quinto
*(**keen**-toh)*
_____

sexto
*(**sehx**-toh)*
_____

séptimo
*(**sehp**-tee-mo)*
_____

octavo
*(ohk-**tah**-voh)*
_____

noveno
*(noh-**veh**-noh)*
_____

décimo
*(**deh**-see-moh)*
_____

Nombre _____

Ordinal Numbers Eleventh to Twentieth
Numeros Ordinales Decimoprimero a Vigésimo

Read the words. Say them aloud. Write the words and say them again as you write them.

decimoprimero
(**deh**-see-moh-
pree-**meh**-roh)   _____

decimosegundo
(**deh**-see-moh
seh-**goon**-doh)   _____

decimotercero
(**deh**-see-moh
tehr-seh-ro))   _____

decimocuarto
(**deh**-see-moh-
kwahr-toh)   _____

decimoquinto
(**deh**-see-moh-
keen-toh)   _____

decimosexto
(**deh**-see-moh-
sehks-toh)   _____

decimoséptimo
(**deh**-see-moh-
sehp-tee-moh)   _____

decimoctavo
(**deh**-see-mohk-
tah-voh)   _____

decimonoveno
(**deh**-see-moh-no-
veh-noh)   _____

vigésimo
(vee-**hehs**-ee-moh))   _____

The Verb To Ride, Walk, Stroll
El Verbo Pasear
(pah-seh-ahr)

Read each sentence. Say it aloud. Write the sentence and say it again as you write it. Write it in English. The first one is done for you.

Yo paseo en mi bicicleta.
(yoh-pah-seh-oh en mee bee-see-kleh-tah)
_____   I ride on my bicycle.

Tú paseas en tu coche
(too-pah-seh-ahs en too koh-cheh)
_____   _____

Usted pasea por avion.
(oo-stehd pah-seh-ah pohr ah-vyohn)
_____   _____

Él pasea a caballo.
(ehl-pah-seh-ah ah kah-bah-yo)
_____   _____

Ella pasea por la casa.
(ehl pah-seh-ah pohr lah kah-sah)
_____   _____

Nosotros paseamos por tren.
(noh-soh-trohs pah-seh-ah-mohs por trehn)
_____   _____

Ustedes pasean por la escuela.
(oo-steh-dehs pah-seh-ahn por lah ehs-kweh-lah)
_____   _____

Ellos pasean a pie.
(eh-yohs pah-seh-ahn ah pee-eh)
_____   _____

Ellas pasean por calle.
(eh-yahs pah-seh-ahn por kah-yeh)
_____   _____

Using the Verb *To Ride, Walk, Stroll*
Usando el Verbo Pasear

Write the correct form of the verb in each sentence. Read it aloud. Draw how people might look while riding or walking in each sentence.

Yo _____ por coche.

Nosotros _____ por barco.

Tú _____ a caballo.

Ellos _____ a pie

Él _____ por taxi.

Ellas _____ por autobús.

Ella _____ por casa.

Ustedes _____ por burro.

Nombre _____

The Verb *To Teach*
El Verbo *Enseñar*

*(ehn-sehn-**yahr**)*

Read each sentence. Say it aloud. Write the sentence and say it again as you write it. Write it in English. The first one is done for you.

Yo enseño
las matemáticas.
*(ehn-**sehn**-yoh lahs
mah-teh-**mah**-tee-kahs)*
_____   I teach math.

Tú enseñas
la geografia.
*(ehn-sehn-**yahs** lah
heh-yoh-grah-**fee**-ah*
_____   _____

Él enseña historia.
*(ehn-**sehn**-yah
ees-**toh**-ree-ah)*
_____   _____

Ella enseña
todos los días (every day).
*(ehn-**sehn**-yah
toh-dohs lahs **dee**-ahs)*
_____   _____

Nosotros enseñamos
a la escuela (school).
*(ehn-**sehn**-yah-mohs)*
_____   _____

Ellos enseñan muchas
estudiantes (many students).
*(ehn-**sehn**-yahn)*
_____   _____

Ellas enseñan en
el parque.
*(**pahr**-keh)*
_____   _____

Ustedes enseñan
deportes (sports).
*(deh-**pohr**-tehs)*
_____   _____

Nombre _____

Using the Verb *To Teach*
Usando el Verbo *Enseñar*

Write the correct form of the verb in each sentence. Read it aloud. Draw a picture showing what is happening in each sentence.

Yo _____ música.	Nosotros _____ todos los días.
Tú _____ las matemáticas.	Ustedes _____ historia.
Él _____ fútbol todas las mañanas.	Ellos _____ en la piscina.
Ella _____ muchas cosas.	Ellas _____ geografía en mi escuela.

To Go and Transportation Review
Repaso del Verbo *Ir* y Transporte

Fill in the missing forms of the verb *ir* and the types of transportation in Spanish to complete each sentence. The first one is done for you.

El niño _____va_____ en el _____carro_____.
(car)

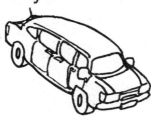

Los niños _____ en el _____.
(taxi)

Nosotros _____ en el _____.
(boat)

_____ vas en los _____.
(skates)

Yo _____ en la _____.
(bicycle)

Ustedes _____ en el _____.
(train)

Las niñas _____ en la _____.
(limousine)

La niña _____ en el _____.
(airplane)

Usted _____ en el _____.
(truck)

Nombre _____

To See and Objects Review #1
Repaso del Verbo *Ver* y Objetos #1

Read each sentence aloud. Draw a picture to show what it means. Write the sentence. The first one is done for you.

Yo veo tres círculos.   ◯ ◯ ◯   _____

Ella ve triángulos rojos.   _____

Nosotros vemos
corazones rosados.   _____

El maestro ve la tiza.   _____

Los abuelos ven
los carros.   _____

La tía ve los trastes.   _____

Las maestras ven
los plátanos.   _____

Las niñas ven
las uvas verdes.   _____

         FS-23102 Spanish—Elementary Level 2

Nombre _____

To See and Objects Review #2
Repaso del Verbo *Ver* y Objetos #2

Read the English and Spanish sentences. Draw a line from each English sentence to the matching Spanish sentence. Read the Spanish sentence aloud.

Yo veo tres círculos.

Ella ve triángulos rojos.

Nosotros vemos
corazones rosados.

El maestro ve la tiza.

Los abuelos ven
los carros.

La tía ve los trastes.

Las maestras ven
la bandera.

Yo veo el avión.

Nosotros vemos
la panadería.

El señor ve el barco.

Los estudiantes ven
el patio de recreo.

Las niñas ven
las flores amarillas.

Tú ves la mano.

La mamá ve los bebés.

The teacher sees the chalk.

We see pink hearts.

The grandfathers see the cars.

She sees red triangles.

I see three circles.

The students see the playground.

The man sees the boat.

The (female) teachers see the flag.

You see the hand.

We see the bakery.

The mom sees the babies.

I see the airplane.

The aunt sees the dishes.

The girls see the yellow flowers.

To Have and Articles Review
Repaso del Verbo *Tener* y Artículos

Read the sentences aloud. Translate the sentences into Spanish and write them on the lines.

1. I have a bicycle.

   _____

2. You have a chair.

   _____

3. He has three cars.

   _____

4. Beth has an apple.

   _____

5. The girls have a cake.

   _____

6. The boys have ice cream.

   _____

7. Cindy has a lollipop.

   _____

8. Bob and Jim have milk.

   _____

9. María has a soda.

   _____

10. I have a tortilla.

   _____

Using Verbs and Articles Review
Repaso de Usando Verbos y Artículos

Write the correct verb and article in Spanish to complete the sentence. Read the sentence aloud. The first one is done for you.

Use the verb (jugar) and the article (el/la).

1. La niña ___juega___ en ___el___ parque.

2. Mary y Sue _____ en _____ jardín.

Use the verb (ir) and the definite article (el/la).

1. _____ maestra _____ a la escuela.

2. Papá y yo _____ a _____ biblioteca.

3. Bob _____ a _____ tienda.

Use the verb (estar) and the indefinite article (un/una).

1. Yo _____ en _____ tienda.

2. _____ niño _____ en la casa.

3. Bob y Frank _____ en _____ cine.

Use the verb (ver) and the plural form of the indefinite article (unas/unos)

1. Cindy y Sam _____ _____ museos.

2. Yo _____ _____ escuelas.

Articles Reference Page
Artículos (the, a/an) Página de Referencia
*(ahr-**tee**-koo-lohs **pah**-hee-nah deh reh-feh-**rehn**-see-ah)*

All nouns are either masculine or feminine in Spanish. When a word ends in **a**, it is classified as feminine. When a word ends is **o**, it is classified as masculine. Most words that end in **-d** and in **-ión** are classified as feminine. When a word ends in letters other than a or o, there is no quick way of knowing which words are masculine and which are feminine.

Definite article (the):

el (ehl)   la (lah)

El is used with a masculine noun.
    The boy is in the store.   **El** niño está en la tienda.
    Maria sees the tree.   María ve **el** árbol.

La is used with a feminine noun.
    The cat has six kittens.   **La** gata tiene seis gatitos.
    Juan sees the fruit.   Juan ve **la** fruta.

Indefinite article (a/an):

    un (oon)   una (**oo**-nah)   unos (**oo**-nohs)   unas (**oo**-nahs)

Un is used with a masculine noun.
    A book is on the table.   **Un** libro está en la mesa.
    A doctor goes to the hospital.   **Un** doctor va al hospital.

Una is used with a feminine noun.
    A girl plays with me.   **Una** niña juega conmigo.
    I see a table.   Yo veo **una** mesa.

Plural Forms
To form plural words add -s to words that end in a vowel (libro/libros, casa/casas) and -es to words that end in a consonant (doctor/doctores, hospital/hospitales).

Plural forms for articles:		singular	plural
el	los	el niño	los niños
la	las	la mesa	las mesas
un	unos	un carro	unos carros
una	unas	una casa	unas casas

Articles Practice
Práctica de Artículos

Fill in the correct Spanish article to complete each sentence. Read the sentence aloud.

Use **el** or **la**

1. _____ tía está en _____ teatro.

2. Me da _____ menú.

3. _____ niño juega en _____ parque.

4. ¿Cómo está _____ abuela?

5. ¿Cómo se llama _____ maestro?

Use **un** or **una**

6. Mamá va a _____ correo.

7. ¿Dónde está _____ banco?

8. _____ doctor (male) va a _____ casa.

9. Papá está en _____ restaurante.

10. Mario ve a _____ secretaria.

Use **unos** or **unas**

11. Me da _____ uvas.

12. Elizabeth ve _____ helados.

Vocabulary Test/Examen del Vocabulario

Circle the best answer.

1. The person who delivers mail is a
   A. bombero   C. plomero
   B. jardinero   D. cartero

2. This person works in a bakery.
   A. piloto   C. panadero
   B. músico   D. peluquero

3. I go here to watch movies.
   A. hotel   C. correo
   B. cine   D. teatro

4. This place has thousands of books.
   A. parque   C. museo
   B. carnicería   D. biblioteca

5. Billy keeps his money in a...
   A. banco   C. salón de belleza
   B. tienda   D. farmacia

6. Which of these vehicles does not belong on land?
   A. tren   C. barco
   B. limosina   D. carro

7. Which of these vehicles can fly?
   A. camión   C. barco de vela
   B. avión   D. nave

8. Find the vehicle that belongs in water.
   A. nave   C. helicóptero
   B. autobús   D. taxi

9. Find the opposite of happy.
   A. cansado   C. triste
   B. enojado   D. feliz

10. Find the word that means sick.
    A. aburrido   C. feliz
    B. enfermo   D. sorprendido

Answer the questions in Spanish.

11. Name a holiday in December.

_____

12. What time do you get up in the morning?

_____

13. What time is your favorite TV program on?

_____

14. How are you?

_____

15. How old are you?

_____

16.-28.

Translate the words below into English.

Spanish	English
yo	_____
estoy	_____
tú	_____
juegas	_____
usted, él, ella	_____
nosotros, nosotras	_____
ustedes, ellos, ellas	_____
ven	_____

Translate the following sentences into Spanish.

29. The girls play in the park.

_____

30. The boy is under the table.

_____

Verbs Test/Examen de los Verbos

Write the correct form of **to go/ir** on each line.

1. Yo _____ a la biblioteca todas las semanas.

2. Tú _____ a la tienda con tu hermana.

3. Él _____ a la escuela todos los días.

4. Nosotros _____ al parque a las tres.

5. Ellas _____ al cine en la noche.

6. Ustedes _____ a jugar a las siete.

Write the correct form of **to see/ver** on each line.

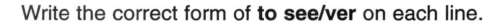

7. Yo _____ con mis ojos.

8. Ella _____ un perro blanco.

9. Nosotros _____ el tren.

10. Ellos _____ dos pájaros.

11. Tú _____ tu gato negro.

12. Ustedes _____ el caballo.

Write the correct form of **to have/tener** on each line.

13. Tú _____ doce años.

14. Nosotros _____ una casa grande.

15. Él _____ orejas pequeñas.

16. Yo _____ dos abuelas.

Articles Test
Examen de los Artículos

Write **el** or **la**, **los** or **las** in front of each noun. Remember that **el** and **la** are used for singular nouns (one) and **los** and **las** are used for plural (more than one) nouns.

1. _____ museo es muy grande.

2. _____ tía esta muy cansada.

3. Voy a _____ bibiloteca por _____ noche.

4. _____ hombre es muy guapo.

5. _____ maestra es delgada.

6. _____ perro es pequeño.

7. Yo paseo en _____ carreta.

8. Mi hermano va a _____ escuela .

9. _____ maestros van a la cafeteria.

10. Ella es _____ cocinera en un restaurante Mexicano.

11. El es _____ veterinario de mi perro.

12. _____ muchachos pasean por motocicleta.

Greetings and Common Phrases Test
Examen de Saludos y Frases Comunes

Translate into Spanish. When a question (pregunta) is written in Spanish an upside-down question mark is placed at the beginning of the sentence and a right-side up one at the end. The first one is done for you.

1. How are you?   ¿Cómo está usted?
   _____

2. Fine, thank you.   _____

3. Good morning.   _____

4. How is your mother?   _____

5. Good evening.   _____

6. Thank you.   _____

7. You're welcome.   _____

8. What is your name?   _____

9. My name is…   _____

10. Where do you live?   _____

11. Where is your friend?   _____

12. Do you want to play?   _____

Nombre _____

Restaurant and Store Test/Examen del Restaurante y de la Tienda

Translate each English sentence into Spanish.

1. May I have the menu? _____

2. I would like a hamburger (hamburguesa). _____

3. Do you have desserts (postres)? _____

4. Where is the restroom? _____

5. May I have the bill please? _____

6. How much does it cost? _____

7. Can you help me? _____

8. Where is the telephone? _____

9. I am just looking. _____

10. I will take it. _____

11. Women (Restroom) _____

12. Men (Restroom) _____

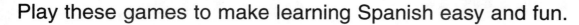

Fun With Spanish

Play these games to make learning Spanish easy and fun.

1. Spanish Stew (Sopa de Vocabulario en Español)
   Make flashcards of 50 Spanish vocabulary words. Draw pictures of each on separate cards. Mix up the cards. Pass out the cards until they're all gone. Each person throws out a card. Everyone takes a turn. The one who matches it takes it. Whoever has the most matches wins the game.

2. Hopscotch and Rope-jumping (Rayuela y Saltar la Cuerda)
   Use Spanish numbers to play hopscotch and count in Spanish when jumping rope. When someone cannot think of the correct number, they lose their turn.

3. Storytime (Cuentos)
   Write a story using vocabulary words from this book on large paper. Challenge students or friends to replace the English nouns with those in Spanish. Illustrate the story with drawings or pictures cut from magazines.

4. Rapid Rabbit (Conejo Rápido)
   Write the names of all the occupations you know in Spanish in three minutes.

5. Name It! (Dale un Nombre)
   Give out blank index cards. Have students or friends write the names of everything they can think of in Spanish in the room you're in and place the cards (one word per card, please) on the object.

6. Spanish Challenge (Reto en Español)
   This is fun to do with partners. Challenge each other to name parts of the body, clothing, and anything else worn or carried. The person who names the most items wins!

Vocabulary

Occupations

baker	el panadero	(pah-nah-**deh**-roh)
banker	el banquero	(bahn-**keh**-roh)
barber/hairdresser	el peluquero	(peh-loo-**keh**-roh)
cook	el cocinero	(koh-see-**neh**-roh)
dentist	el/la dentista	(den-**tees**-tah)
doctor	el doctor	(dohk-**tohr**)
engineer	el ingeniero	(een-heh-**nee-eh**-roh)
firefighter	el bombero	(bohm-**beh**-roh)
gardener	el jardinero	(har-dee-**neh**-roh)
jeweler	el joyero	(ho-**yeh**-roh)
lawyer	el abogado	(ah-boh-**gah**-doh)
librarian	el bibliotecario	(bee-bleeoh-teh-**kah**-ree-yoh)
milkman	el lechero	(leh-**cheh**-roh)
musician	el músico	(**moo**-see-koh)
pharmacist	el farmacéutico	(fahr-mah-**seh**-oo-tee-koh)
pilot	el piloto	(pee-**loh**-toh)
plumber	el plomero	(ploh-**meh**-roh)
policeman	la policía	(poh-lee-**see**-yah)
postman	el cartero	(kar-**teh**-roh)
secretary	la secretaria	(seh-kreh-**tah**-ree-yah)
veterinarian	el veterinario	(veh-teh-ree-**nah**-ree-yoh)

Community

bakery	la panadería	(lah pah-nah-deh-**ree**-yah)
bank	el banco	(ehl **bahn**-koh)
barber shop	la peluquería	(lah peh-loo-keh-**ree**-yah)
beauty salon	el salón de belleza	(ehl sah-**lohn** deh beh-**yeh**-sah)
church	la iglesia	(lah ee-**glehs**-ee-yah)
drugstore	la farmacia	(lah fahr-**mah**-see-yah)

fire station	la estación de bomberos	*(lah ehs-tah-**syohn** deh bohm-**beh**-rohs)*
hospital	el hospital	*(ehl ohs-pee-**tahl**)*
hotel	el hotel	*(ehl oh-**tehl**)*
library	la biblioteca	*(lah bee-blee-oh-**teh**-kah)*
meat market	la carnicería	*(lah kahr-nee-seh-**ree**-yah)*
movie theater	el cine	*(ehl **see**-neh)*
museum	el museo	*(ehl moo-**seh**-oh)*
park	el parque	*(ehl **pahr**-keh)*
post office	el correo	*(ehl koh-**reh**-oh)*
restaurant	el restaurante	*(ehl rehs-tah-oo-**rhan**-teh)*
shoe store	la zapatería	*(lah sah-pah-teh-**ree**-yah)*
store	la tienda	*(lah tee-**ehn**-dah)*
supermarket	el supermercado	*(ehl soo-pehr-mehr-**kah**-doh)*
theater	el teatro	*(ehl teh-**ah**-troh)*
zoo	el zoológico	*(ehl soh-**loh**-hee-koh)*

Transportation

airplane	el avión	*(ehl ah-**vyohn**)*
bicycle	la bicicleta	*(lah bee-see-**kleh**-tah)*
boat	el barco	*(ehl **bahr**-koh)*
bus	el autobús	*(ehl ah-toh-**boos**)*
car	el carro	*(ehl **kah**-roh)*
helicopter	el helicóptero	*(ehl eh-lee-**kohp**-teh-roh)*
limousine	la limosina	*(lah lee-moh-**see**-nah)*
motorcycle	la motocicleta	*(lah moh-toh-see-**kleh**-tah)*
sailboat	el barco de vela	*(ehl **bahr**-koh deh veh-lah)*
scooter	el patinete	*(ehl pah-tee-**neh**-teh)*
ship	la nave	*(lah **nah**-veh)*
skateboard	la patineta	*(lah pah-tee-**neh**-tah)*
skates	los patines	*(lohs pah-**tee**-nehs)*
spaceship	la nave espacial	*(lah **nah**-veh ehs-pah-**seeyal**)*
submarine	el submarino	*(ehl soob-mah-**ree**-noh)*

taxi	el taxi	*(ehl **tahk**-see)*
train	el tren	*(ehl trehn)*
truck	el camión	*(ehl kah-**myohn**)*
wagon	la carreta	*(lah kah-**reh**-tah)*

Holidays and Celebrations

birthday	el cumpleaños	*(ehl koom-pleh-**ah**-nyohs)*
Christmas	la Navidad	*(lah nah-vee-**dahd**)*
Christmas Eve	la Nochebuena	*(lah noh-cheh-**bweh**-nah)*
Easter	la Pascua	*(lah **pahs**-kwah)*
Father's Day	el Día de los Padres	*(ehl **dee**-ah deh lohs **pah**-drehs)*
Independence Day	el Día de la Independencia	*(ehl **dee**-ah deh lah een-deh-pehn-**dehn**-see-ah)*
Mother's Day	el Día de las Madres	*(ehl **dee**-ah deh lahs **mah**-drehs)*
New Year	el Año Nuevo	*(ehl **ah**-nyoh **nueh**-voh)*
Saint Patrick's Day	el Día de San Patricio	*(ehl **dee**-ah deh sahn pah-**tree**-syoh)*
Thanksgiving Day	el Día de Acción de Gracias	*(ehl **dee**-ah deh ahk-see-**ohn** deh **grah**-see-ahs)*
Valentine's Day	el Día de San Valentín	*(ehl **dee**-ah deh sahn vah-lehn-**teen**)*

Prepositional Phrases

above	sobre/encima de	*(**soh**-breh/ehn-**see**-mah deh)*
behind	detrás de	*(deh-**trahs** deh)*
below	debajo de	*(deh-**bah**-hoh deh)*
beneath	bajo	*(**bah**-hoh)*
between	entre	*(**ehn**-treh)*
in	en	*(ehn)*
in back	detrás de	*(deh-**trahs** deh)*
in front	delante de	*(deh-**lahn**-teh deh)*
inside	dentro de	*(**dehn**-troh deh)*
on	en	*(ehn)*
outside of	fuera de	*(**fweh**-rah deh)*

| over | sobre/ por encima de | (**soh**-breh/pohr **ehn**-see-mah deh) |
| under | debajo de | (deh-**bah**-hoh deh) |

Personal Pronouns

he	él	(ehl)
I	yo	(yoh)
she	ella	(**eh**-yah)
they, feminine	ellas	(**eh**-yahs)
they, masculine	ellos	(**eh**-yohs)
we	nosotros	(noh-**soh**-trohs)
you, familiar	tú	(too)
you, formal	usted	(oos-**tehd**)
you, plural	ustedes	(oos-**teh**-dehs)

Present Tense Verbs

to be	estar	(**ehs**-tahr)
to go	ir	(eer)
to have	tener	(teh-**nehr**)
to play	jugar	(hoo-**gahr**)
to see	ver	(vehr)

Feelings and Emotions

angry	enojado	(eh-noh-**hah**-doh)
bored	aburrido	(ah-boo-**ree**-doh)
busy	ocupado	(oh-koo-**pah**-doh)
happy	feliz	(feh-**lees**)
sad	triste	(**trees**-teh)
scared	asustado	(ah-soos-**tah**-doh)
sick	enfermo	(ehn-**fehr**-moh)
surprised	sorprendido	(sohr-prehn-**dee**-doh)
tired	cansado	(kahn-**sah**-doh)
worried	preocupado	(preh-oh-koo-**pah**-doh)

Articles

a/an, feminine	una	*(**oo**-nah)*
a/an, feminine, plural	unas	*(**oo**-nahs)*
a/an, masculine	un	*(oon)*
a/an, masculine, plural	unos	*(**oo**-nohs)*
the, feminine	la	*(lah)*
the, feminine, plural	las	*(lahs)*
the, masculine	el	*(ehl)*
the, masculine, plural	los	*(lohs)*

Physical Descriptions

bad	malo/a	*(**mah**-loh/lah)*
beautiful	bello/a	*(**beh**-yoh/yah)*
big	grande	*(**grahn**-de)*
fast	rápido/a	*(**rah**-pee-doh/dah)*
fat	gordo/a	*(**gohr**-doh/dah)*
good	bueno/a	*(**bueh**-noh/nah)*
good-looking	guapo/a	*(**gooah**-poh/pah)*
medium	mediano/a	*(meh-**deeah**-noh/nah)*
old	viejo/a	*(vee-**eh**-hoh/hah)*
pretty	bonito/a	*(boh-**nee**-toh/tah)*
pretty	lindo/a	*(**leen**-doh/dah)*
short	bajo/a	*(**bah**-hoh/hah)*
slow	lento/a	*(**lehn**-toh/tah)*
small	pequeño/a	*(peh-**keh**-nyoh/nyah)*
tall	alto/a	*(**ahl**-toh/tah)*
thin	delgado/a	*(dehl-**gah**-doh/dah)*
ugly	feo/a	*(**feh**-oh/ah)*
young	joven	*(**hoh**-vehn)*

Answer Key

Nombre _____

Occupations/Las Ocupaciones

Finish the following sentences. Write the correct occupation on each line in English (inglés) and in Spanish (español).

	English/inglés	Spanish/español
After the plane landed, I got to meet the	pilot	piloto
Cindy had a toothache. She went to the	dentist	dentista
Joe had the mumps. He went to the	doctor	doctor
Becky's sink broke. She called a	plumber	plomero
The bridge was built by an	engineer	ingeniero
We gave our mail to the	mail carrier	cartero
Dan loves the guitar. He wants to be a	musician	músico
My dad likes to make pastries. That's why he became a	baker	panadero
Ralph likes to put out fires. He is a	firefighter	bombero
Marc gave me a great haircut. He is a wonderful	barber	peluquero

Page 4

Nombre _____

Occupations and Places/Ocupaciones y Lugares

Write each occupation to match the work places.

Ocupaciones

1. el hospital — el doctor
2. la biblioteca — el bibliotecario
3. el correo — el cartero
4. la farmacia — el farmacéutico
5. el zoológico — el veterinario
6. el salón de belleza — el peluquero
7. el teatro — el músico
8. el restaurante — el cocinero
9. el banco — el banquero
10. la estación de bomberos — el bombero
11. el panadería — el panadero

Page 7

Nombre _____

Word Search

The Community/La Comunidad

(lah koh-moo-nee-dahd)

Find and circle the Spanish words hidden in the puzzle. Translate the words into English.

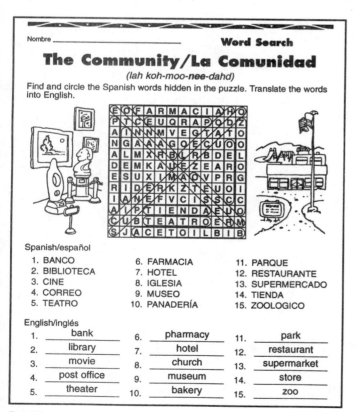

Spanish/español
1. BANCO
2. BIBLIOTECA
3. CINE
4. CORREO
5. TEATRO
6. FARMACIA
7. HOTEL
8. IGLESIA
9. MUSEO
10. PANADERÍA
11. PARQUE
12. RESTAURANTE
13. SUPERMERCADO
14. TIENDA
15. ZOOLOGICO

English/inglés
1. bank
2. library
3. movie
4. post office
5. theater
6. pharmacy
7. hotel
8. church
9. museum
10. bakery
11. park
12. restaurant
13. supermarket
14. store
15. zoo

Page 8

Nombre _____

Occupations and Community Review
Repaso de Ocupaciones y Comunidad

Write, in Spanish, the places in the community that go with the occupations listed.

Occupation Ocupacion	Places in the Community Lugares en la comunidad
1. peluquero	la peluquería
2. banquero	el banco
3. cocinero	el restaurante
4. farmacéutico	la farmacia
5. jardinero	el parque
6. cartero	el correo
7. músico	el teatro
8. doctor	el hospital
9. bibliotecario	la biblioteca
10. veterinario	el zoológico

Page 9

Answer Key

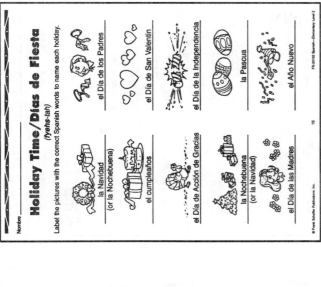

Holiday Time/Días de Fiesta
(fyeh-stah)

Label the pictures with the correct Spanish words to name each holiday.

la Navidad
(or la Nochebuena)

el Día de San Valentín

el cumpleaños

el Día de la Independencia

el Día de Acción de Gracias

la Pascua

la Nochebuena
(or la Navidad)

el Día de los Padres

el Día de las Madres

el Año Nuevo

Page 16

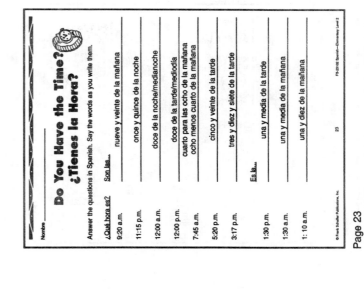

Do You Have the Time?/¿Tienes la Hora?

Answer the questions in Spanish. Say the words as you write them.

¿Qué hora es?	Son las...
9:20 a.m.	nueve y veinte de la mañana
11:15 p.m.	once y quince de la noche
12:00 a.m.	doce de la noche/medianoche
12:00 p.m.	doce de la tarde/mediodía
7:45 a.m.	cuarto para las ocho de la mañana / ocho menos cuarto de la mañana
5:20 p.m.	cinco y veinte de la tarde
3:17 p.m.	tres y diez y siete de la tarde
	Es la...
1:30 p.m.	una y media de la tarde
1:30 a.m.	una y media de la mañana
1:10 a.m.	una y diez de la mañana

Page 23

Transportation Everywhere
Transporte en Todas Partes
(trahns-pohr-teh ehn toh-dahs pahr-tes)

Write the correct Spanish words for the kinds of transportation that can be used in each place.

(ocean)

el barco — el submarino

el barco de vela — la nave

(land)

el carro — el autobús

el tren — la camión

la bicicleta — la motocicleta

los patines — la patineta

la carreta — el patinete

la limosina — el taxi

(air)

el avión — el helicóptero

la nave espacial

Page 13

Hidden Words/Palabras Escondidas
(pah-lah-brahs ehs-kohn-dee-dahs)

Find and circle the Spanish words hidden in the puzzle. Write each word in English.

Spanish	English
1. ADIÓS	goodbye
2. CÓMO	how
3. CUANDO	when
4. DAMAS	women
5. DÓNDE	where
6. GRACIAS	thank you
7. HOLA	hello

Spanish	English
8. HOMBRES	men
9. MENÚ	menu
10. NO	no
11. QUÉ	what
12. QUIÉN	who
13. SÍ	yes

Page 21

Vehicles/Vehículos
(vee-hee-koo-lohs)

Use the clues to help you name each vehicle. Write the words in English and in Spanish on the lines. Don't forget to include el or la.

Clues Pistas *(peece-tahs)*	English word Palabra en inglés	Spanish word Palabra en español
two wings, flies	airplane	el avión
two wheels, handlebars	bicycle	la bicicleta
four wheels, big	truck	el camión
floats, ocean, lake, small	sailboat	el barco de vela
four wheels, family transportation	car	el carro
two wheels, motor	motorcycle	la motocicleta
six wheels, passengers, fare	bus	el autobús
flies, propeller	helicopter	el helicóptero
many wheels, track	train	el tren
eight wheels, pair	skates	los patines

Page 12

A New Friend/Un Amigo Nuevo
(oon ah-mee-go nueh-voh)

Write the following conversation in Spanish:

Susan: Good morning, Mark.

Buenos días, Mark.

Mark: Hello, Susan. How are you?

Hola, Susan ¿Como está usted?

Susan: Fine, thank you.

Bien, gracias.

Mark: How old are you?

¿Cuántos años tiene?

Susan: I am ten years old.

Tengo diez años.

Mark: Do you want to play?

¿Quiere jugar?

Susan: Yes. Thank you.

Sí. Gracias.

Page 20

FS-23102 Spanish—Elementary Level 2

Answer Key

Writing Prepositions/Escribiendo las Preposiciones
(ehs-kree-byehn-doh)

Look at each picture. Write the correct preposition in Spanish.

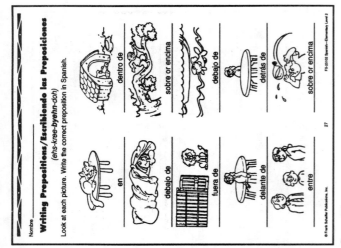

en
dentro de
debajo de
sobre or encima
fuera de
debajo de
delante de
detrás de
entre
sobre or encima

How Do You Feel?/¿Como Se Siente?
(koh-meh seh see-ehn-teh)

Read each sentence. Say it aloud. Write it and say it again as you write it. Translate each sentence into English. The first one is done for you.

El niño está cansado. — The boy is tired.
Nosotros estamos tristes. — We are sad.
La niña está cansada. — The girl is tired.
Tú estás enfermo. — You are sick.
Yo estoy feliz. — I am happy.
Ustedes están preocupados. — You are worried.
Ellos están enojados. — They are angry.
Usted está ocupado. — You are busy.
Ellas están enojadas. — They are angry.

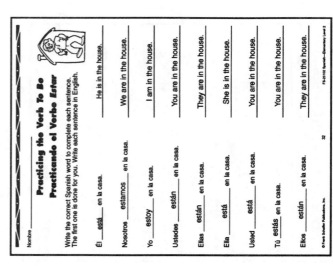

Preposition Practice/Práctica de Preposiciones
(preh-poh-see-see-oh-nehs)

Read the phrase in Spanish. Each one is called a prepositional phrase. Say it aloud. Match the phrase to the picture by drawing lines between the pairs.

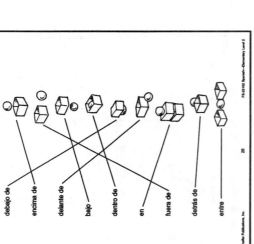

debajo de
encima de
delante de
bajo
dentro de
en
fuera de
detrás de
entre

Practicing the Verb To Be/Practicando el Verbo Estar

Write the correct Spanish word to complete each sentence. The first one is done for you. Write each sentence in English.

El **está** en la casa. — He is in the house.
Nosotros **estamos** en la casa. — We are in the house.
Yo **estoy** en la casa. — I am in the house.
Ustedes **están** en la casa. — You are in the house.
Ellas **están** en la casa. — They are in the house.
Ella **está** en la casa. — She is in the house.
Usted **está** en la casa. — You are in the house.
Tú **estás** en la casa. — You are in the house.
Ellos **están** en la casa. — They are in the house.

It's About Time/¿A Qué Hora?
(ah-keh-oh-rah)

Answer the questions below in Spanish. Remember to write morning, afternoon, or night.

Answers will vary.

What time do you get up in the morning?

What time do you have breakfast?

What time do you go to school or work?

What time do you have lunch?

What time do you get home?

What time do you eat dinner?

What time do you go to bed?

Pronoun Matching/Emparejando los Pronombres
(ehm-pah-rah-hahn-doh lohs proh-nohm-brehs)

Draw a line between each matching pair of pronouns in English and Spanish.

ellos — we
usted — you, plural
él — I
ustedes — she
nosotros — they, feminine
ella — you, formal
yo — he
tú — they, masculine
ellas — you, familiar

Answer Key

Pronouns and the Verb To Play
Pronombres y El Verbo *Jugar*

Nombre _____

Write the correct form of *jugar* to complete each sentence. The first one is done for you.

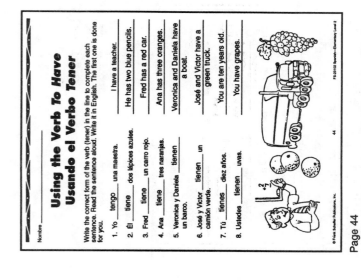

Yo __juego__ en el parque.

Ella __juega__ en el parque.

Nosotros __jugamos__ en el parque.

Usted __juega__ en el parque.

Ellos __juegan__ en el parque.

Ellas __juegan__ en el parque.

Ustedes __juegan__ en el parque.

Tú __juegas__ en el parque.

Él __juega__ en el parque.

© Frank Schaffer Publications, Inc.

Page 38

Using the Verb To Have
Usando el Verbo *Tener*

Nombre _____

Write the correct form of the verb (tener) in the line to complete each sentence. Read the sentence aloud. Write it in English. The first one is done for you.

1. Yo __tengo__ una maestra. — I have a teacher.
2. Él __tiene__ dos lápices azules. — He has two blue pencils.
3. Fred __tiene__ un carro rojo. — Fred has a red car.
4. Ana __tiene__ tres naranjas. — Ana has three oranges.
5. Veronica y Daniela __tienen__ un barco. — Veronica and Daniela have a boat.
6. José y Victor __tienen__ un camión verde. — José and Victor have a green truck.
7. Tú __tienes__ diez años. — You are ten years old.
8. Ustedes __tienen__ uvas. — You have grapes.

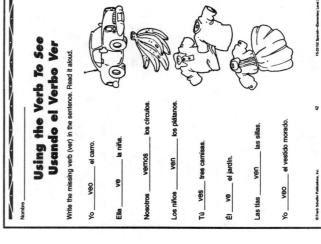

© Frank Schaffer Publications, Inc.

Page 44

Using the Verb To Play/Usando el Verbo *Jugar*

Nombre _____

Look at the pictures. Write a sentence in Spanish using the verb jugar to show what is happening in each picture.

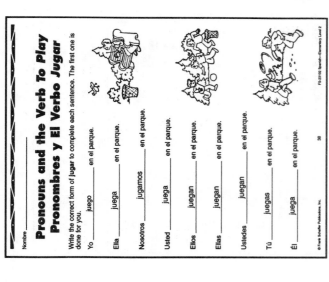

Ella juega en el parque.

Ellas juegan en la casa.

Ellas juegan en el parque.

Nosotros jugamos en el parque.
or Ellos juegan en el parque.

Nosotros jugamos en el parque.
or Ellos juegan en el parque.

Él juega en el parque.

Yo juego en la casa.

Yo juego en el parque.
or El juego en el parque.

Ellas juegan en el parque.

© Frank Schaffer Publications, Inc.

Page 37

Using the Verb To See
Usando el Verbo *Ver*

Nombre _____

Write the missing verb (ver) in the sentence. Read it aloud.

Yo __veo__ el carro.

Ella __ve__ la niña.

Nosotros __vemos__ los círculos.

Los niños __ven__ los plátanos.

Tú __ves__ tres camisas.

Él __ve__ el jardín.

Las tías __ven__ las sillas.

Yo __veo__ el vestido morado.

© Frank Schaffer Publications, Inc.

Page 42

Writing About Feelings
Escribiendo Sobre los Sentimientos
(*soh-breh sehn-tee-myehn-tohs*)

Nombre _____

Write the missing Spanish words.

El niño __está__ cansado.
_is_

La mamá está __feliz__.
happy

Nosotros __estamos ocupados__.
_We_

Las niñas __están__ tristes.
are

Yo __estoy sorprendido__.
_I_

Ustedes __están__ enojados.
are

La niña está __asustado__.
scared

Yo estoy __sorprendido__.
surprised

Nosotros __estamos__ enfermos.
are

Tú __estás__ preocupado.
are

Tú / Usted __estás preocupada__.
You

© Frank Schaffer Publications, Inc.

Page 35

Using the Verb To Go
Usando el Verbo *Ir*

Nombre _____

Write Spanish sentences on the lines to show the correct order in which the girls are going to each place. Use the verb ir (to go).

1-restaurant   5-store
2-bank   6-movie theater
3-park   7-library
4-bakery   8-supermarket

1. Ellas van al restaurante. — They go to the restaurant.
2. Ellas van al banco. — They go to the bank.
3. Ellas van al parque. — They go the park.
4. Ellas van a la panadería. — They go to the bakery.
5. Ellas van a la tienda. — They go to the store.
6. Ellas van al cine. — They go to the movies.
7. Ellas van a la biblioteca. — They go to the library.
8. Ellas van al supermercado. — They go to the supermarket.

© Frank Schaffer Publications, Inc.

Page 40

Answer Key

Prepositional Phrases Review
Repaso de Frases Preposicionales

Read the English sentences and write the Spanish words that are missing. The first one is done for you.

The vase is on the table. El vaso está __en__ la mesa.

Dad is behind mom. El papá está __detrás de__ la mamá.

Dad is in front of Grandma. El papá está __delante de__ la abuela.

The lollipop is in my mouth. La paleta está __en__ mi boca.

Uncle is between the girls. El tío está __entre__ las niñas.

The girl is outside the house. La niña está __fuera de__ la casa.

Grandpa is inside the house. El abuelo está __dentro de__ la casa.

The jacket is over the shirt. La chaqueta está __sobre__ la camisa.

The restaurant is above the library. El restaurante está __encima de__ la biblioteca.

The book is under the desk. El libro está __debajo de__ el escritorio.

The paper is under the hand. El papel está __debajo de__ la mano.

Page 47

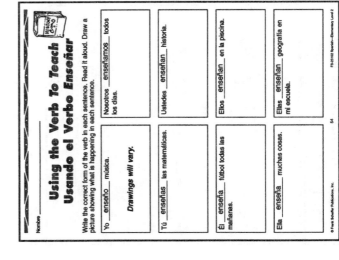

Using the Verb *To Teach*
Usando el Verbo *Enseñar*

Write the correct form of the verb in each sentence. Read it aloud. Draw a picture showing what is happening in each sentence.

Yo __enseño__ música.

Drawings will vary.

Tú __enseñas__ las matemáticas.

Él __enseña__ fútbol todas las mañanas.

Ella __enseña__ muchas cosas.

Nosotros __enseñamos__ todos los días.

Ustedes __enseñan__ historia.

Ellos __enseñan__ en la piscina.

Ellas __enseñan__ geografía en mi escuela.

Page 54

Common Phrases Review
Repaso de Frases Comunes

Write a conversation for the following scene:

You have just met your friend for lunch at a restaurant. Greet him/her and ask the waiter for a menu. Order your meal and make sure you include a protein, a vegetable, a fruit, and a beverage. Ask for the bill, and say good-bye to your friend.

Answers will vary.

Page 46

Using the Verb *To Ride, Walk, Stroll*
Usando el Verbo *Pasear*

Write the correct form of the verb in each sentence. Read it aloud. Draw how people might look while riding or walking in each sentence.

Yo __paseo__ por coche.

Drawings will vary.

Tú __paseas__ a caballo.

Él __pasea__ por taxi.

Ella __pasea__ por casa.

Nosotros __paseamos__ por barco.

Ellos __pasean__ a pie.

Ellas __pasean__ por autobús.

Ustedes __pasean__ por burro.

Page 52

Verb Practice
Práctica con los Verbos

Read each English sentence. Fill in the blanks with the correct Spanish words. Read each sentence aloud.

1. I see the house. Yo __veo__ la __casa__.

2. He plays in the garden. Él __juega__ en el __jardín__.

3. Mom goes to the store. Mamá __va__ a la __tienda__.

4. Dad is in the museum. Papá __está__ en el __museo__.

5. Cindy plays with Sam. Cindy __juega__ con Sam.

6. She sees the classroom. Ella __ve__ el __aula__.

7. Frank goes to the library. Frank __va__ a la __biblioteca__.

8. The girl is in the bank. La niña __está__ en el __banco__.

9. Mom and Dad go to the movies. Mamá y papá __van__ al __cine__.

10. We see the school. Nosotros __vemos__ la __escuela__.

Write each sentence in Spanish. Say it as you write it.

1. I see an apple. __Yo veo una manzana.__

2. Mom goes to the market. __Mamá va a la tienda.__

3. Bob is in the restaurant. __Bob está en el restaurante.__

Page 45

Prepositions Crossword Puzzle
Crucigrama de Preposiciones

Write the words in Spanish in the spaces.

Across
1. over
2. inside
3. in back
4. outside of

Down
5. below
6. above
7. in front
8. behind
9. in
10. beneath
11. between

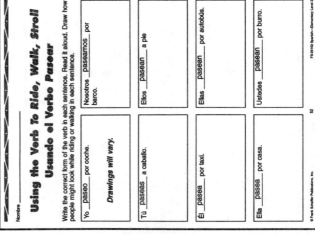

Page 48

FS-23102 Spanish—Elementary Level 2

Answer Key

79

Page 57

Nombre

To See and Objects Review #2
Repaso del Verbo Ver y Objetos #2

Read the English and Spanish sentences. Draw a line from each English sentence to the matching Spanish sentence. Read the Spanish sentence aloud.

Yo veo tres círculos.	The teacher sees the chalk.
Ella ve triángulos rojos.	We see pink hearts.
Nosotros vemos corazones rosados.	The grandfathers see the cars.
El maestro ve la tiza.	She sees red triangles.
Los abuelos ven los carros.	I see three circles.
La tía ve los trastes.	The students see the playground.
Las maestras ven la bandera.	The man sees the boat.
Yo veo el avión.	The (female) teachers see the flag.
Nosotros vemos la panadería.	You see the hand.
El señor ve el barco.	We see the bakery.
Los estudiantes ven el patio de recreo.	The mom sees the babies.
Las niñas ven las flores amarillas.	I see the airplane.
Tú ves la mano.	The aunt sees the dishes.
La mamá ve los bebés.	The girls see the yellow flowers.

57

© Frank Schaffer Publications, Inc.   FS-23102 Spanish—Elementary Level 2

Page 61

Nombre

Articles Practice
Práctica de Artículos

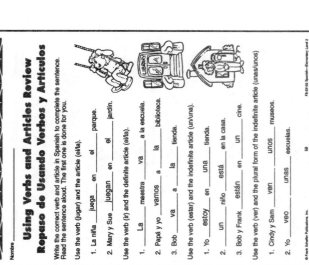

Fill in the correct Spanish article to complete each sentence. Read the sentence aloud.

Use el or la

1. La __la__ tía está en __el__ teatro.
2. Me da __el__ menú.
3. __El__ niño juega en __el__ parque.
4. ¿Cómo está __la__ abuela?
5. ¿Cómo se llama __el__ maestro?

Use un or una

6. Mamá va a __un__ correo.
7. ¿Dónde está __un__ banco?
8. __El__ doctor (male) va a __una__ casa.
9. Papá está en __un__ restaurante.
10. Mario va a __una__ secretaria.

Use unos or unas

11. Me da __unas__ uvas.
12. Elizabeth ve __unos__ helados.

61

© Frank Schaffer Publications, Inc.   FS-23102 Spanish—Elementary Level 2

Page 56

Nombre

To See and Objects Review #1
Repaso del Verbo Ver y Objetos #1

Read each sentence aloud. Draw a picture to show what it means. Write the sentence. The first one is done for you.

Yo veo tres círculos.   ◯ ◯ ◯   I see three circles.

Ella ve triángulos rojos.   _____ She sees red triangles.

Nosotros vemos corazones rosados.   _____ We sink pink hearts.

El maestro ve la tiza.   _____ The teacher sees chalk.

Los abuelos ven los carros.   _____ The grandfathers see cars.

La tía ve los trastes.   _____ The aunt sees the dishes.

Las maestras ven los plátanos.   _____ The teachers see bananas.

Las niñas ven las uvas verdes.   _____ The girls see green grapes.

56

© Frank Schaffer Publications, Inc.   FS-23102 Spanish—Elementary Level 2

Page 59

Nombre

Using Verbs and Articles Review
Repaso de Usando Verbos y Artículos

Write the correct verb and article in Spanish to complete the sentence. Read the sentence aloud. The first one is done for you.

Use the verb (jugar) and the article (el/la).

1. La niña __juega__ en __el__ parque.
2. Mary y Sue __juegan__ en __el__ jardín.

Use the verb (ir) and the definite article (el/la).

1. La maestra __va__ a __la__ escuela.
2. Papá y yo __vamos__ a __la__ biblioteca.
3. Bob __va__ a __la__ tienda.

Use the verb (estar) and the indefinite article (un/una).

1. Yo __estoy__ en __una__ tienda.
2. __un__ niño __está__ en la casa.
3. Bob y Frank __están__ en __un__ cine.

Use the verb (ver) and the plural form of the indefinite article (unas/unos).

1. Cindy y Sam __ven__ __unos__ museos.
2. Yo __veo__ __unas__ escuelas.

59

© Frank Schaffer Publications, Inc.   FS-23102 Spanish—Elementary Level 2

Page 55

Nombre

To Go and Transportation Review
Repaso del Verbo Ir y Transporte

Fill in the missing forms of the verb Ir and the types of transportation in Spanish to complete each sentence. The first one is done for you.

El niño __va__ en el __carro__ . (car)

Los niños __van__ en el __taxi__ . (taxi)

Nosotros __vamos__ en el __barco__ . (boat)

Tú __vas__ en los __patines__ . (skates)

Yo __voy__ en la __bicicleta__ . (bicycle)

Ustedes __van__ en el __tren__ . (train)

Las niñas __van__ en la __limosina__ . (limousine)

La niña __va__ en el __avión__ . (airplane)

Usted __va__ en el __camión__ . (truck)

55

© Frank Schaffer Publications, Inc.   FS-23102 Spanish—Elementary Level 2

Page 58

Nombre

To Have and Articles Review
Repaso del Verbo Tener y Artículos

Read the sentences aloud. Translate the sentences into Spanish and write them on the lines.

1. I have a bicycle.
   Yo tengo una bicicleta.
2. You have a chair.
   Tú tienes una silla.
3. He has three cars.
   El tiene tres carros.
4. Beth has an apple.
   Beth tiene una manzana.
5. The girls have a cake.
   Las niñas tienen un pastel.
6. The boys have ice cream.
   Los niños tienen helado.
7. Cindy has a lollipop.
   Cindy tiene una paleta.
8. Bob and Jim have milk.
   Bob y Jim tienen leche.
9. María has a soda.
   María tiene una soda.
10. I have a tortilla.
    Yo tengo una tortilla.

58

© Frank Schaffer Publications, Inc.   FS-23102 Spanish—Elementary Level 2

Answer Key

Vocabulary Test/Examen del Vocabulario

Nombre _____

Circle the best answer.

1. The person who delivers mail is a
   A. bombero   C. plomero
   B. jardinero   **D. cartero**

2. This person works in a bakery.
   A. piloto   **C. panadero**
   B. músico   D. peluquero

3. I go here to watch movies.
   A. hotel   C. correo
   B. cine   D. teatro

4. This place has thousands of books.
   A. parque   **C. museo**
   B. carnicería D. biblioteca

5. Billy keeps his money in a...
   A. banco   C. salón de belleza
   B. tienda   D. farmacia

6. Which of these vehicles does not belong on land?
   A. tren   **C. barco**
   B. limosina   D. carro

7. Which of these vehicles can fly?
   A. camión   **C. barco de vela**
   B. avión   D. nave

8. Find the vehicle that belongs in water.
   A. nave   C. helicóptero
   B. autobús   D. taxi

9. Find the opposite of happy.
   A. cansado   **C. triste**
   B. enojado   D. feliz

10. Find the word that means sick.
    A. aburrido   C. feliz
    B. enfermo D. sorprendido

Answer the questions in Spanish.

11. Name a holiday in December.
    Navidad or Nochebuena

12. What time do you get up in the morning?
    Answers will vary.

13. What time is your favorite TV program on?
    Answers will vary.

Page 62

---

14. How are you?
    Bien, gracias.

15. How old are you?
    Tengo _____ años. (Answers will vary)

16.–28. Translate the words below into English.

Spanish	English
yo	I
estoy	am
tú	you
juegas	play
usted, él, ella	you, he, she
nosotros, nosotras	we
ustedes, ellos, ellas	you, they
ven	see

Translate the following sentences into Spanish.

29. The girls play in the park.
    Las niñas juegan en el parque.

30. The boy is under the table.
    El niño está debajo de la mesa.

Page 63

Verbs Test/Examen de los Verbos

Nombre _____

Write the correct form of **to go/ir** on each line.

1. Yo ___voy___ a la biblioteca todas las semanas.
2. Tú ___vas___ a la tienda con tu hermana.
3. Él ___va___ a la escuela todos los días.
4. Nosotros ___vamos___ al parque a las tres.
5. Ellas ___van___ al cine en la noche.
6. Ustedes ___van___ a jugar a las siete.

Write the correct form of **to see/ver** on each line.

7. Yo ___veo___ con mis ojos.
8. Ella ___ve___ un perro blanco.
9. Nosotros ___vemos___ el tren.
10. Ellos ___ven___ dos pájaros.
11. Tú ___ves___ tu gato negro.
12. Ustedes ___ven___ el caballo.

Write the correct form of **to have/tener** on each line.

13. Tú ___tienes___ doce años.
14. Nosotros ___tenemos___ una casa grande.
15. Él ___tiene___ orejas pequeñas.
16. Yo ___tengo___ dos abuelas.

Page 64

Articles Test
Examen de los Artículos

Nombre _____

Write **el** or **la**, **los** or **las** in front of each noun. Remember that **el** and **la** are used for singular nouns (one) and **los** and **las** are used for plural (more than one) nouns.

1. __El__ museo es muy grande.
2. __La__ tía esta muy cansada.
3. Voy a __la__ biblioteca por __la__ noche.
4. __El__ hombre es muy guapo.
5. __La__ maestra es delgada.
6. __El__ perro es pequeño.
7. Yo paseo en __la__ carreta.
8. Mi hermano va a __la__ escuela.
9. __Los__ maestros van a la cafetería.
10. Ella es __la__ cocinera en un restaurante Mexicano.
11. __El__ es __el__ veterinario de mi perro.
12. __Los__ muchachos pasean por motocicleta.

Page 65

Greetings and Common Phrases Test
Examen de Saludos y Frases Comunes

Nombre _____

Translate into Spanish. When a question (pregunta) is written in Spanish an upside-down question mark is placed at the beginning of the sentence and a right-side up one at the end. The first one is done for you.

1. How are you?   ¿Cómo está usted?
2. Fine, thank you.   Bien, gracias.
3. Good morning.   Buenos días.
4. How is your mother? ¿Cómo está su madre?
5. Good evening.   Buenas noches.
6. Thank you.   Gracias.
7. You're welcome.   De nada.
8. What is your name?   ¿Cómo se llama?
9. My name is...   Me llamo
10. Where do you live? ¿Dónde vive?
11. Where is your friend? ¿Dónde está su amigo?
12. Do you want to play? ¿Quiere jugar?

Page 66

Restaurant and Store Test/Examen del Restaurante y de la Tienda

Nombre _____

Translate each English sentence into Spanish.

1. May I have the menu?   ¿Me da el menú?
2. I would like a hamburger (hamburguesa). Me gustaría una hamburguesa.
3. Do you have desserts (postres)? ¿Tiene postres?
4. Where is the restroom?   ¿Dónde está el baño?
5. May I have the bill please? ¿Me da la cuenta?
6. How much does it cost?   ¿Cuánto cuesta?
7. Can you help me?   ¿Me puede ayudar?
8. Where is the telephone?   ¿Dónde está el teléfono?
9. I am just looking.   Sólo estoy mirando.
10. I will take it.   Me lo llevo.
11. Women (Restroom)   Damas
12. Men (Restroom)   Caballeros/Hombres

Page 67

25 Terrific Art Projects
Based on
Favorite Picture Books

by Karen Backus, Linda Evans, and Mary Thompson

SCHOLASTIC
PROFESSIONAL BOOKS

New York • Toronto • London • Auckland • Sydney
Mexico City • New Delhi • Hong Kong • Buenos Aires

■ ■

We dedicate this book to the authors and illustrators who inspired these art projects.

Cover design by Andrew Jenkins

Interior illustrations by Cary Pillo

Interior design by Sydney Wright

Edited by Gaye-Taylor Upchurch

ISBN: 0-439-22263-X

Copyright © 2002 by Karen Backus, Linda Evans, and Mary Thompson.

All rights reserved.

Printed in the U.S.A.

6 7 8 9 10   40   08 07 06 05

Contents

Introduction

The thrill and anticipation experienced when opening a new book or revisiting a favorite story is one of life's great pleasures for those who love to read. We can take a journey to new worlds and adventures or follow fictional friends through familiar problems. Through reading, our imagination is stretched and expanded, and by observing illustrations, particularly those in children's books, our creativity and expression are explored and developed.

Our editor, Deborah Schecter, encouraged us to explore the connection between favorite children's books and art activities—an exciting idea for three elementary art educators! We have shared many wonderful children's books with our students and have enjoyed their excitement as they create art inspired by their reading. In this book we couple favorite children's books with a variety of art activities to pique children's interest in both art and reading. The activities are designed to introduce a variety of art materials and techniques as well as new art terms and concepts appropriate for young children.

Encourage children to be "art detectives" and discover what medium or materials an illustrator has used. Search for clues in the pictures. (Many books include a brief explanation of the materials used.) We have also included information on the illustrator's style to help children gain an awareness of different styles and mediums. Using class time to observe and discuss what is alike and what is different in illustrations will encourage visual literacy and critical thinking in young children.

With so many wonderful children's books out there, we feel this selection is just the tip of the iceberg. We hope this book will inspire children to look more closely at illustrations and to make the connection between art and literature as they continue their reading adventures.

Helpful Hints

Preparation

* A few steps of preparation can prevent disasters. In advance, plan the cleanup procedure for each project. A consistent routine will make this step easier for all! Children love to help, and with a little direction you'll have a quick, effective cleanup.

* In advance, gather supplies and cut paper to the size specified for each activity. (The paper size does not need to be exact.) Save valuable hands-on time by setting up materials before children arrive.

✱ Always try an art activity yourself before presenting it to children. Your experience will serve you well in anticipating any problems that might arise. As you go through the steps, think of simple ways to explain what you are doing. Also, having a completed example to show children will help them understand the activity and will pique their interest.

✱ To save time, paper, and erasers, have children first practice drawing a shape with their finger on the paper or in the air. This step lets you check for understanding and offer help in working out potential problems.

✱ If artwork needs to dry, plan ahead for a place to put it. A clothesline and clothespins may work where space is limited.

✱ If students are easily distracted or are eager to begin and don't wait for directions, distribute the art supplies on an "as needed" basis.

✱ If desired, play music that relates to the activity or evokes a mood appropriate for the project.

✱ Before children begin a project, have them write their names on the back of their papers.

✱ Encourage experimentation! Children may be more at ease if you are doing the activity simultaneously and learning along with them. Sharing your own struggles may also help some children feel more comfortable when attempting something new.

Introducing a Project

✱ Introduce children to artistic terms that may be unfamiliar to them. For each activity, you'll find a short list of words that will be helpful for children to know as they engage in the activity. These words are highlighted the first time they appear in the activity.

✱ The sections entitled Let's Begin provide more specific ideas for introducing each project.

✱ For inspiration, discuss and observe illustrations in the selected book.

✱ Children often need suggestions about where to place shapes on their paper. Be specific when giving directions. For example, telling young children to draw large isn't enough information. If you want children to draw a figure that fills the paper, demonstrate how to begin near the top of the paper and draw the head. Then explain that the feet should be drawn at or near the bottom. Don't skip this simple step: A little time spent on information about placement on the paper will affect the entire composition and the success of children's artwork!

Drawing

* Several lessons in this book refer to the "look and draw" technique, a step-by-step method of drawing that works well with young children. The object is not to have the children's art be a copy of yours but rather to help them succeed in executing the activities. This method is especially useful for helping children position objects in particular places on their paper.

  When using this method, position yourself in a spot where every child can see you. Draw a few lines at a time, have children observe, and then have them follow your example. Keep in mind that the beauty of children's artwork lies in their unique way of seeing the world. Look for ways to encourage their originality and to help them express their ideas.

Painting

* Put tempera paints on foam trays or paper plates for easy cleanup.

* Use garbage bags to cover work surfaces. Cut off the bottom of a bag and slit one side; then tape it to the sides of a table. You can wipe off the garbage bag cover and reuse it if desired.

* Paint smocks are the best insurance for hassle-free painting. Men's short-sleeved T-shirts or button-down shirts worn backward offer great coverage.

* To clean tempera paint off paintbrushes, soak the paintbrushes for ten minutes in water with a little dishwashing soap. The paint will rinse off easily.

Displaying Children's Work

* Children love to see their artwork displayed. The time it takes to set up a display is well worth it!

* How artwork is displayed can make the difference between "so-so" and "wow!" viewer responses. The section accompanying each project entitled Art Show offers specific suggestions for displaying each of the projects. Try out your own ideas, and encourage students to contribute theirs as well.

* A simple way to mount artwork starts with a little planning. For a painting activity, give students paper that has been trimmed an inch on each side. For example, if you would like to mount a project that calls for 12- by 18-inch paper, trim the paper so that it's 11 inches by 17 inches. You can then glue the painting onto 12- by 18-inch paper to create a border. Use large background paper to unify your displays and help avoid the distraction of wall color or patterns.

Papa, Please Get the Moon for Me

by Eric Carle

Create a whimsical collage using paint, craft sticks, and paper scraps.

Let's Begin

Read aloud *Papa, Please Get the Moon for Me* to the class. Ask children to close their eyes and imagine a moonlit sky. Ask: "What colors do you see? What shapes do you see? Does the moon ever seem large enough to reach out and touch?" Describe how you might climb and touch something that is out of reach.

Show children a real ladder or a picture of a ladder (you might sketch one for them). Notice how the ladder's rungs create a **pattern**, and observe how the ladder can illustrate **balance**.

Cover work surfaces to prepare for painting, and pass out the materials. Then demonstrate the following procedures as children follow along.

Step by Step

1. Place a sheet of white paper in a **vertical** position. Using an easel brush dipped in blue paint, drag the paintbrush horizontally across the width of the paper for a smooth stroke of color. Dip the same brush into the white paint and lightly **overlap** the first line. The paint will mix on the paper and create a new **value**, or lightness, of blue. Continue back-and-forth brush strokes using the blue and white paint alternately until the entire paper is filled with different values of blue. Let the painting dry.

New Art Words

pattern overlap
balance value
vertical collage

 ## Materials

* ladder or picture of a ladder
* 9- by 24-inch white paper
* easel paintbrush
* tempera paint (blue and white)
* water containers
* craft sticks
* glue
* paper scraps (yellow, gray, and white)
* scissors
* markers or crayons
* blue or black paper (optional, for mounting)

2. Recall the ladder children observed and the discussion about pattern and balance. Arrange the craft sticks on the dry painting to construct a ladder. Remember to check for balance and pattern before gluing the sticks into place. Once the ladder has been glued into place, the artwork is called a **collage**. A collage is made by gluing a variety of materials to a surface.

3. Cut out moon and star shapes from yellow and gray scraps of paper. Glue them onto the background.

4. Using a marker or crayon, illustrate a simple human figure on a white scrap of paper. Cut out the figure and glue it onto the ladder.

Bookshelf

One Step More

A science lesson about the phases of the moon works well in conjunction with this art project. Children might also enjoy using their imagination to discover other ways they might reach the moon. Have them illustrate these new ideas.

Art Show

Mount the finished collage on dark paper. Display the projects with written text of the children's comments about the moon. If new ways to reach the moon have been illustrated, display these along with an explanation.

There Was an Old Lady Who Swallowed a Fly

by Simms Taback

illustrated by Pam Adams

The rhyming verse of this silly song inspires funny, exaggerated drawings using crayons and watercolor paints.

Let's Begin

Read aloud *There Was an Old Lady Who Swallowed a Fly* to the class. This story is taken from a song by the same name. Children enjoy learning the song as well as looking at other books based on this story (see Bookshelf). Show children a few versions and ask them to compare them. Point out that each story begins with the same idea but uses different pictures or words to tell the story. Ask children if they think this story is true.

Use this opportunity to observe and discuss what an **illustrator** does. An illustrator uses his or her imagination to tell a story through pictures. Each illustrator thinks of his or her own special way of telling a story.

Cover work surfaces to prepare for painting, and pass out the materials. Then demonstrate the following procedures as children follow along.

Step by Step

1. Place a sheet of white paper in a vertical position. Near the top of the paper, draw a *U* shape in pencil for the woman's head. Leave a little space above the head for a hat. Demonstrate several

New Art Words

illustrator
exaggerate
crayon resist

 ## Materials

* 12- by 18-inch white paper
* pencils
* 8- by 8-inch white paper
* black crayons or black permanent markers
* crayons
* watercolor paints
* paintbrushes
* water containers
* scissors
* glue
* 12- by 18-inch colored paper

different types of hats. Encourage children to create their own original hat design.

2. Draw facial features. Encourage children to create a face that shows expression. They might add glasses to the drawing.

3. Draw the woman's dress. **Exaggerate** its size by making it fill most of the remaining paper. Leave a little space near the bottom for her shoes. Draw arms and hands that look as if they are resting on the woman's stomach. Add sleeves on the arms.

4. Demonstrate a few ideas for shoes. Draw the old woman's two shoes poking out from the bottom of her dress.

5. Add details to the old woman's clothing. Some ideas include collars, ruffles, buttons, and patterns such as polka dots, plaids, or flowers.

6. With a pencil, draw a fly in the middle of a sheet of 8- by 8-inch white paper. Draw a spider around the fly, so that it looks like the fly is in the spider's stomach. Following the story, draw a bird around the spider and a cat around the bird. Continue adding animals from the story until only a few inches of space remain around the drawing.

TIP  For very young children, simplify this step by having them draw only a few animals.

7. Trace over the pencil lines on both drawings by pressing heavily with black crayon (or use black permanent marker). Color parts of both drawings with crayons.

8. Paint both drawings using watercolors. In this **crayon-resist** technique, the wax of the crayon will push away the water of the paints and create an interesting effect.

When painting the animal drawing, leave a few inches around the drawing white. Let the paintings dry.

 **TIP** — To keep the drawings clear, use little or no black and brown paint. If these colors are necessary, use more water and less paint than usual.

9. Cut out the animals, leaving a few inches of white around the drawing.

10. Cut out the lady. Carefully cut out the arms. Glue the figure onto the 12- by 18-inch colored paper, positioned vertically. Glue the animal drawing onto her stomach. Then glue the arms so that the hands rest on the stomach.

One Step More

As a group, examine illustrations of this story to determine similarities and differences between each one. On a large sheet of craft paper, create a Venn diagram to show the similarities and differences.

Art Show

Display children's paintings with the Venn diagram. Gather books that represent the various versions of this story and display them along with the art projects.

Bookshelf

Down by the Bay (Raffi Songs to Read) (Crown Publishing Group, 1999)

I Know an Old Lady Who Swallowed a Fly by Nadine Bernard Westcott (Little, Brown & Company, 1980)

I Know an Old Lady Who Swallowed a Pie by Alison Jackson (Penguin Putnam Books for Young Readers, 1997)

There Was an Old Lady Who Swallowed a Fly by Simms Taback (Child's Play of England, 1989)

There Was an Old Lady Who Swallowed a Trout! by Terri Sloat (Henry Holt & Company, 1998)

New Art Words

overlap
contrasting
self-portrait
border
patchwork

 ## Materials

* 10- by 16-inch dark-colored paper
* white and colored chalk
* paintbrushes
* tempera paints (four colors)
* water containers
* 4- by 8-inch paper in various skin tones
* crayons and markers
* scissors
* glue
* wallpaper and/or fabric in various patterns, cut into 2-inch squares
* 12- by 18-inch white paper

Tar Beach

by Faith Ringgold

Children create a city scene with a flying self-portrait as they take an imaginary journey.

Let's Begin

Read aloud *Tar Beach* to the class. Faith Ringgold's family lives in a city where the coolest place they can find is on the flat roof of their apartment building. Ask: "What does your family do in the summer when it's really hot?" Explain that as a child, the author imagined flying over the city, pretending that she owned the buildings and the Brooklyn Bridge. Ask: "What would you like to fly over and make your own? It might be an ice cream shop, a pet store, the library, or the zoo. What other imaginary journeys could you take?"

Cover work surfaces to prepare for painting, and pass out the materials. Then demonstrate the following procedures as children follow along.

Step by Step

1. Using white chalk on a sheet of dark-colored paper, draw various-sized buildings to create a city scene. The skyline should extend about halfway up the paper. To make it look like a crowded city, draw the buildings so that they touch and **overlap**.

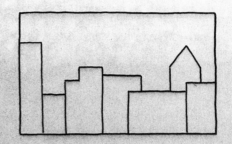

2. Using tempera paint, paint the buildings. Make sure that the buildings that touch each other are different colors. Let the painting dry.

3. Use colored chalk to draw the doors, windows, and signs on the buildings. To make these details stand out, use **contrasting** colors; for example, dark colors show up best on top of light colors (blue on yellow), and light colors show up best on top of dark colors (yellow on black).

4. Use white chalk to add stars and any other extra details (perhaps a bridge) to complete the night scene.

5. Choose a sheet of 4- by 8-inch paper. Use crayons and markers to draw a **self-portrait** in a flying position. Look at the book's illustrations for ideas about what a flying position might look like. Draw and color a favorite outfit.

 **TIP** Use the whole paper by drawing the feet touching one end of the paper and the top of the head or outstretched arms touching the other end.

6. Cut out the flying figure and glue it to the city scene.

7. Explain that you will create a **border** with a **patchwork** design. Glue the wallpaper or fabric squares around the edges of the 12- by 18-inch

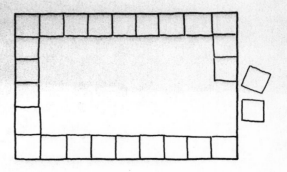

  Bookshelf

Amazing Grace by Mary Hoffman (Dial Books for Young Readers, 1991)

Cassie's Colorful Day by Faith Ringgold (Random House Books for Young Readers, 1999)

A Chair for My Mother by Vera B. Williams (Greenwillow Books, 1982)

My Dream of Martin Luther King by Faith Ringgold (Crown Publishers, 1998)

Tar Beach by Faith Ringgold (Crown Publishers, Inc., 1991)

white paper. Glue the city scene on top of the white paper so that the border frames the picture.

 **TIP** Center the city scene so that an even width of patchwork border is showing on all four sides.

One Step More

Have children write a story about where they would go and what they would see if they could fly.

Art Show

Display children's stories with their city scenes and flying self-portraits.

"My House"

A House Is a House for Me

by Mary Ann Hoberman

Children observe architecture and geometric shapes to illustrate their own homes; then they use the crayon-resist painting technique and add a self-portrait!

Let's Begin

Read aloud *A House Is a House for Me* to the class. The detailed illustrations explore **habitats** of humans, animals, and things. Ask: "What is a habitat? What does your habitat look like?" Have children describe the designs of their homes or homes they have seen. Think about geometric shapes found in homes, such as squares, triangles, rectangles, circles, and ovals. Ask children to think about the details of a house or apartment building. Explain that children will pretend to be **architects** and design a home for themselves. It can be the home they live in or an imaginary home.

New Art Words

habitat
architect
landscaping
crayon resist
patterns

Materials

* 12- by 18-inch white paper
* crayons
* watercolor paints
* paintbrushes
* water containers
* 9- by 12-inch light-colored paper
* pencils
* markers
* scissors
* glue
* black paper (optional, for mounting)

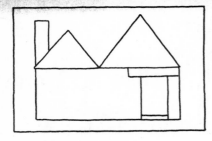

Bookshelf

A House Is a House for Me by Mary Ann Hoberman (Viking Press, 1978)

How a House Is Built by Gail Gibbons (Holiday House, 1990)

The Napping House by Audrey and Don Wood (Harcourt Children's Books, 2000)

So Many Circles, So Many Squares by Tana Hoban (Greenwillow Books, 1998)

Step by Step

1. Select a dark crayon and draw the shape of a home on the 12- by 18-inch paper. Use a variety of shapes, keeping them large and simple.

2. Still using a crayon, draw smaller shapes to represent details of your house such as shutters, shingles, wood, brick, and so on. Use simple shapes for drawing the buildings, houses, or **landscaping** that surrounds your home.

3. Using plenty of water and a brush, paint a wash of watercolor on top of the crayon drawing. When using this **crayon-resist** technique, the wax of the crayon will resist the paint so that the details in the drawing will show. Children can use different colors of paint for different areas of the drawing.

4. Use a pencil to draw a self-portrait on the light-colored paper. Keep the shape simple so it will be easy to cut out.

5. Use markers to create interesting **patterns** on your clothing. Color the drawing with crayons. Cut out and glue the self-portrait onto the house drawing.

One Step More

Share real architectural drawings and house plans with children. Have children design an interior view or floor plan of their home.

Art Show

Mount the projects on black paper. Display the homes and self-portraits to create a classroom neighborhood. Street names and house numbers may be added.

In the Small, Small Pond

by Denise Fleming

Children create a small pond scene using chalk pastels and a sponge-printing technique.

Let's Begin

Read aloud *In the Small, Small Pond* to the class. Ask children to look for the frog image that repeats throughout the story. Invite them to visualize a close-up view of a small pond. Notice the shape of the lily pads. Ask: "How many wings does a dragonfly have? What colors, plants, and reptiles might you see in a pond?"

Cut pieces of sponge or foam into long oval pieces to use for printing dragonfly wings. Three sizes are needed to create the body, the top wings, and the

New Art Words

horizontal
blend
impression
print

Materials

* 12- by 18-inch light-blue paper
* colored chalk or pastels
* paper towels
* sponge or foam cut into ovals and half-circles
* tempera paints (black, white, green, and red)
* paintbrushes
* water containers
* cotton swabs
* 2- by 18-inch strips of green paper (optional, for display)

bottom wings (4 inches, 3 inches, and 2½ inches long and ¾ inch wide). Cut a 3-inch circle in half to print a frog's head. If desired, experiment with different shapes to illustrate pond life.

Cover work surfaces to prepare for painting, and pass out the materials. Then demonstrate the following procedures as children follow along.

Step by Step

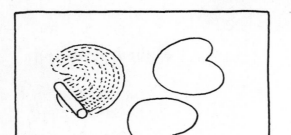

1. Place a sheet of paper in a **horizontal** position. Using the book illustrations as a guide, draw a simple lily pad. Place a piece of yellow chalk on its side and rotate the chalk in a circular motion. Leave a little opening on one side. Draw two or more lily pads.

2. Use a piece of blue chalk and go over the yellow chalk with the same circular motion. Combining these colors produces a soft green color. Wrap a paper towel around two fingers and gently **blend** the chalk.

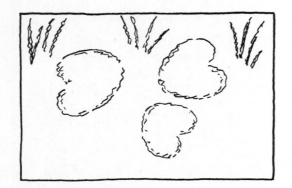

3. Color the background with blue and purple chalk. The combination of these colors creates shadows in the water. Remind children to apply only a small amount of chalk. Blend the colors with a paper towel.

4. Use green chalk to draw grass near the top of the paper.

5. Select the longest oval-shaped sponge and paint one side black. Place it paint-side down on the chalk drawing. Gently pat or press the sponge to make an **impression**. This will

print the dragonfly's body. Repeat to print another dragonfly's body.

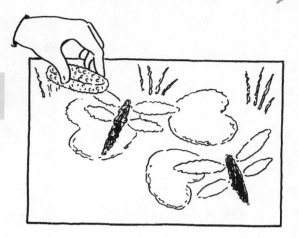

 **TIP** Do not put too much paint on the sponge—it will distort the image.

6. Use white paint on the medium and small ovals to print the top and bottom sets of wings.

7. Using green paint and the half-circle, print a frog's head.

8. Dip cotton swabs in red paint and add eyes to the dragonflies and frog. Add patterns along the dragonflies' bodies. Let the paint dry.

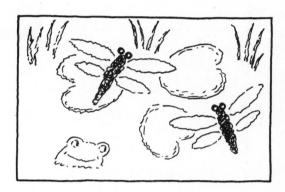

One Step More

The famous French artist Claude Monet painted water lilies growing in a pond. Show examples of his work. Compare and contrast Monet's paintings with Denise Fleming's illustrations.

Art Show

Attach the strips of green paper to the tops and bottoms of the pond scene. Display all the art projects on green or blue background paper to create a large pond scene. Add reproductions of Monet's water lily paintings to the display.

 **Bookshelf**

Blue Frogs: The Second Adventure in John's Colorful World by Margaret S. Campilonga (Chicken Soup Press, 1996)

Frogs, Toads, Lizards and Salamanders by Nancy Winslow Parker and Joan R. Wright (Greenwillow, 1990)

In the Small, Small Pond by Denise Fleming (Holt, 1993)

The Salamander Room by Anne Mazer (Knopf, 1994)

New Art Words

color spectrum
overlap
composition
collage

 Materials

- * real flowers or pictures of flowers
- * pencils
- * 4- by 4-inch squares of colored paper (red, orange, yellow, light green, blue, violet)
- * scissors
- * glue
- * 12- by 18-inch white paper
- * scraps of green paper
- * 1/2- by 10-inch strips of green paper
- * pictures from seed catalogs
- * black paper (optional, for mounting)

Planting a Rainbow

by Lois Ehlert

Children learn about the color spectrum by creating a garden on paper.

Let's Begin

Read aloud *Planting a Rainbow* to the class. Discuss the colors of the rainbow. Introduce children to the correct order of a rainbow **color spectrum** (red, orange, yellow, green, blue, indigo, and violet: ROY G. BIV). Explain that indigo will not be used in this project. After observing Ehlert's illustrations, help children identify the different shapes of flower petals. Look for ovals, circles, diamonds, triangles, and stars. Display real flowers or pictures for inspiration.

Pass out the materials. Then demonstrate the following procedures as children follow along.

Step by Step

1. On the paper squares, draw a variety of simple flower shapes that fill the paper. Encourage children to use large, simple shapes for the flowers and to use all colors.

 **TIP** If drawings are too small to cut out, flowers can easily be enlarged. Just add another outline around the first drawing.

2. Cut out the flowers. Use the scraps to make centers for the flowers.

3. Glue the flowers near the top of the white paper in the order of the spectrum (red, orange, yellow, green, blue, and violet). **Overlap** the flowers to make a pleasing **composition**, or arrangement.

4. Draw various simple leaf shapes on the scraps of green paper. Cut out the leaves. Glue a stem at the base of each flower, tucking it under the flower. Glue the leaves to complete the rainbow garden **collage**.

One Step More

Look through seed catalogs and magazines to find pictures of real flowers in the colors of the spectrum. Arrange and glue the pictures in the correct spectrum order to create a rainbow garden poster.

Art Show

Mount the completed gardens on black paper to show off the bold colors. Display the rainbow gardens with pictures of rainbows that show the color spectrum. Display the rainbow garden poster nearby.

Bookshelf

All the Colors of the Rainbow (Rookie Read-About Science) by Allan Fowler (Children's Press, 1999)

Growing Colors by Bruce McMillan (Lothrop, Lee & Shepard, 1988)

Planting a Rainbow by Lois Ehlert (Harcourt Brace Jovanovich, 1988)

What Makes a Rainbow? by Betty Ann Schwartz (Intervisual Books, 2000)

New Art Words

composition   shadow
overlapping   highlight
pattern   depth

Materials

- 9- by 12-inch green paper
- pencils
- Craypas
- pictures of tropical plants and animals
- 12- by 18-inch white paper
- scissors
- glue
- 12- by 18-inch colored paper

The Great Kapok Tree: A Tale of the Amazon Rain Forest

by Lynne Cherry

Children draw colorful patterns on rain forest animals and plants in this project that combines art and science.

Let's Begin

Read aloud *The Great Kapok Tree: A Tale of the Amazon Rain Forest* to the class. Discuss the conservation of the tropical rain forests and the animals that are in danger of extinction. Notice the illustrator's pleasing arrangement, or **composition**, of **overlapping** leaves, plants, and animals on each page. Observe the **patterns** on the animals and plants.

Pass out the materials. Then demonstrate the following procedures as the children follow along.

Step by Step

1. On the green paper, use a pencil to draw several rain forest leaves. Draw large leaves that touch the edges of the paper. Make some leaves larger than others. Then draw patterns on the leaves.

2. Color the leaves using blue Craypas to emphasize **shadows** and yellow Craypas to emphasize **highlights**. With dark green Craypas, add lines for the leaf veins.

3. After looking through the picture references, select a tropical animal to illustrate. On the white paper, use a pencil to draw a simple sketch of the animal. Use simple shapes such as large ovals for the head, body, and legs. Explain that showing only part of the animal can create an interesting composition.

4. Select one color at a time to draw a pattern on the animal, such as spots or stripes.

5. Cut out the leaves and the animal.

6. Arrange the drawings on a sheet of 12- by 18-inch paper to create an interesting composition. Glue the drawings into place.

TIP

Slightly overlapping the drawings will create an illusion of **depth**.

Bookshelf

Amazon Alphabet by Martin and Tanis Jordan (Larousse Kingfisher Chambers, 1996)

Animals Brightly Colored by Phyllis L. Tildes (Charlesbridge Publishing, 1998)

The Great Kapok Tree: A Tale of the Amazon Rain Forest by Lynne Cherry (Harcourt Brace Jovanovich, 1990)

How the Animals Got Their Colors: Animal Myths From Around the World by Michael Rosen (Harcourt Children's Books, 1992)

A Walk in the Rainforest by Kristen Joy Pratt (Dawn, 1992)

One Step More

The famous artist Henri Rousseau used plants from French gardens to inspire his junglelike paintings. Show and discuss examples of his work.

Art Show

Create a Rain Forest Survival display. Place artwork around a large tree cut out of paper. For a three-dimensional effect, twist brown craft paper for vines and staple green leaves to the display. On strips of paper, write facts about the rain forest that students have learned; add these facts to the display.

I like to make snowballs.

The Snowy Day

by Ezra Jack Keats

Children use paper and fabric to make a collage depicting themselves in a snowy scene.

Let's Begin

Read aloud *The Snowy Day* to the class. Ezra Jack Keats's illustrations are **collages** created with torn and cut papers, fabric, and paint. In *The Snowy Day*, a young boy experiences the beauty of newly fallen snow. Ask: "What do you like to do in the snow? What special clothes do you need to wear? How does it feel to be so bundled up? How does the cold feel on your face? What sounds do your feet make as they walk?" Look at photographs or pictures of snow and snowflakes. Notice the special beauty of snowflakes in the book's illustrations, and point out that each snowflake is unique.

New Art Words

collages
horizontal
composition

Materials

* pictures of snow and snowflakes
* 12- by 18-inch blue paper
* white cotton or polyester batting
* glue
* white chalk or crayons
* felt or other fabric (various colors)
* scissors
* scraps of colored and black paper
* fine-tip markers or crayons
* 2- by 9-inch white paper
* 18- by 24-inch colored paper (optional, for mounting)

TIP

Good scissors will be essential for children's success when cutting felt and fabric.

Pass out the materials. Then demonstrate the following procedures as children follow along.

Step by Step

1. Place a sheet of blue paper in a **horizontal** position.

2. Tear sections of white cotton or polyester batting for the snow. Arrange the batting on the paper to create piles of snow on the ground. After creating a **composition**, or arrangement that is pleasing, glue the batting onto the paper. The snow should cover the bottom half of the page and should stretch from one side of the paper to the other.

3. Use white chalk or crayons to draw several snowflakes of various shapes and sizes. Be sure that each snowflake is unique.

4. Add a self-portrait wearing winter clothing to the scene. For the clothing, cut felt or fabric into small rectangular shapes to make the body of a jacket, long sleeves, and pant legs. Arrange the rectangles to create an outfit on the paper, and glue them into place. Cut details such as pockets, mittens, and buttons from smaller scraps of felt.

5. For the face, draw a circle on a scrap of paper. Using fine-tip markers or crayons, draw eyes, a nose, hair, and a mouth. Cut out the face and glue it into place.

6. Draw a hat on a scrap of felt or fabric and cut it out. Glue the hat into place.

7. Cut out boots from black paper scraps and glue them into place.

8. Using fabric or paper scraps, add other details to the snow scene, such as the sun or a snowman. Or you might draw these details.

One Step More

On a strip of white paper, have each child write something he or she likes to do on a snowy day.

Art Show

Mount the collages and statements on 18- by 24-inch sheets of colored paper. Have children cut out paper snowflakes. Surround children's snowy day pictures with cutouts of snowflakes.

Bookshelf

Axle Annie by Robin Pulver (Dial Books for Young Readers, 1999)

Dream Snow by Eric Carle (Philomel Books, 2000)

Kipper's Snowy Day by Mick Inkpen (Harcourt Brace, 1996)

Snow by Uri Shulevitz (Farrar, Straus & Giroux, 1998)

Snow Day by Moira Fain (Walker Publishing Company, 1996)

The Snowy Day by Ezra Jack Keats (Viking Press, 1962)

White Snow, Bright Snow by Alvin Tressalt (Lothrop, Lee & Shepard, 1988 ©1947)

Draw Me a Star

by Eric Carle

Create a garden with finger paintings, using Eric Carle's textured-paper technique.

Let's Begin

Read aloud *Draw Me a Star* to the class. Note the variety of **textures** that author-illustrator Eric Carle uses in his illustrations. Ask: "How can texture be created on wet paint?" Explain that Carle's illustrations are examples of **collage** because they are made up of a variety of materials glued onto a surface. Remind students that when using **finger paint**, colors may be mixed to create new colors: red + blue = purple; yellow + blue = green; red + yellow = orange.

Materials

* 6- by 9-inch finger paint paper
* spoons
* finger paint (green and other bright colors)
* tubs of water
* old combs, forks, and cardboard scraps
* spray bottle of water
* 12- by 18-inch white or light-colored construction paper
* scissors
* glue
* dark-colored paper (optional, for mounting)

TIP  Before passing out the finger paint, demonstrate how to use it.

Cover work surfaces to prepare for painting. Then demonstrate the following procedures as children follow along.

Step by Step

1. Distribute three sheets of finger paint paper to each child. Before painting, place each sheet of finger paint paper on newspaper. This makes it easier to move the painted papers to a drying area without tearing them.

2. Place a teaspoon of green paint on one sheet. Place a teaspoon of a different color paint on each of the other two sheets. With your fingers, spread the paint to the outer edges of the paper. Encourage students to mix two colors together to create a new color (see Let's Begin).

3. Use your fingers or the side of your hand to create textured patterns in the paint. Carefully scrape combs, forks, or pieces of cardboard over the paper to create different textures. If the paint becomes dry, lightly spray it with water. Then let the paintings dry.

 **TIP**
Before working with a different paint color, rinse fingers in tubs of water placed at each table.

4. Show examples of collage from the story, particularly the flower garden collages. Cut stems and leaves from green textured papers and cut tulips or other flower shapes from the other textured papers. Encourage children to share papers so that each flower garden will have a wide range of colors and textures.

 **TIP**
The tulip shape is simply a *U* shape with a zigzag cut at the top. Explore other flower shapes; magazines and old greeting cards are a good source of various flower pictures.

5. Overlap the flowers to create a pleasing arrangement, or **composition**, on the 12- by 18-inch paper. Glue the garden into place.

One Step More

Eric Carle is famous for including a sun in his collage stories. Children may want to cut out and add a sun to their artwork. Small butterflies and insects may also be added to the garden. Combine the art project with a science lesson by studying specific types of butterflies, insects, birds, and other animals that might be attracted to a flower garden.

Art Show

Mount the finished collages on larger sheets of colored paper and display the flower gardens to create a field of flowers. Display the Eric Carle book with the collages. Or, instead of making individual collages, glue textured paper onto craft or butcher paper to create a giant flower garden mural!

Bookshelf

Alison's Zinnia by Anita Lobel (Greenwillow Books, 1990)

The Art of Eric Carle by Eric Carle (Philomel Books, 1996)

Draw Me a Star by Eric Carle (Philomel, 1992)

Fairy Dusters and Blazing Stars: Exploring Wildflowers With Children by Suzanne M. Samson (Roberts Rinehart, 1994)

Grandma's Purple Flowers by Adjoa J. Burrowes (Lee & Low Books, 2000)

Plant Book: Starting With Nature by Pamela Hickman (Turtleback Books, 2000)

The Tiny Seed by Eric Carle (Simon & Schuster, 2001)

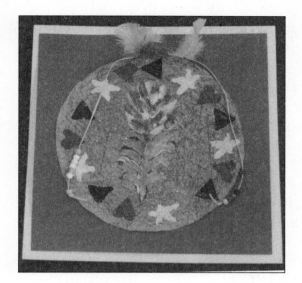

New Art Words

printmaking
pattern
overlap

The Legend of the Indian Paintbrush

by Tomie dePaola

Inspired by the Native American legend of the paintbrush flower, children create a shield design on "leather-like" brown paper.

Let's Begin

Read aloud *The Legend of the Indian Paintbrush* to the class. Discuss how this Native American legend explains the origin of something in nature. Observe the bright colors of the paintbrush flower and how they resemble the colors of the sunset. Ask children if they can think of any other legends that explain something that occurs in nature.

Native Americans painted colorful shield designs on leather. The shields were believed to protect the owner with special powers.

 ## Materials

- ✷ brown paper grocery bags (or heavy brown wrapping paper)
- ✷ bowl or sink
- ✷ newspapers or towels
- ✷ brown crayons, unwrapped
- ✷ 11-inch circle template
- ✷ pencils
- ✷ scissors
- ✷ tempera paint (green, red, and yellow)
- ✷ paper plates
- ✷ objects for printing (spools, cotton swabs, wood blocks, and cut sponges)
- ✷ paintbrushes
- ✷ water containers
- ✷ glue
- ✷ feathers, yarn or string, and beads
- ✷ brightly colored or black paper (optional, for mounting)

In advance, cut the sides of the brown bags so that they open up as a flat piece of paper. Then cut the bag in half, so that each bag will make two shields. If using brown wrapping paper, cut it into 12- by 12-inch sheets. Copy and cut out enough circle templates for children to share. Pour a few inches of water into a large bowl or sink. Have newspapers or towels on hand.

Cover work surfaces to prepare for painting, and pass out the materials. Then demonstrate the following procedures as children follow along.

Step by Step

1. Soak a brown bag or piece of wrapping paper in the water for 2–3 seconds. Gently squeeze out excess water by rolling the paper loosely into a ball shape. Gently open it up and lay it flat on a newspaper or towel to dry. The wrinkles in the paper simulate the leather of a Native American shield.

2. After the paper has dried, rub it with the side of an unwrapped brown crayon. This will give the paper a textured look like leather.

3. Trace the 11-inch circle onto the brown paper. Cut out the circle and explain that it will be a shield.

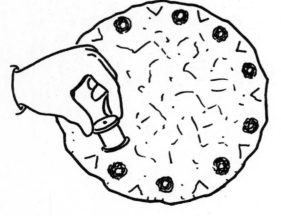

4. Pour the paints into paper plates. Model how to use the objects for **printmaking**. Dip an object in paint. (Use an extra plate to hold the wet printing objects.) Press the object onto the shield. Show children how to make a **pattern** by printing a repeating sequence of two or three objects. Print a pattern along the edge of the circle. Let the paint dry.

Further illustrate the idea of a pattern by assigning each object a letter of the alphabet, such as "A-B-C." Then say "A-B-C, A-B-C" as you stamp the shapes in that sequence.

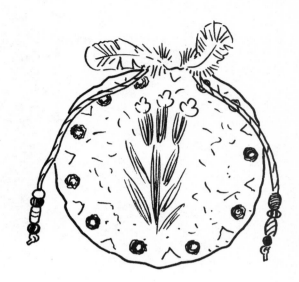

5. Paint a paintbrush flower in the middle of the circle. Use green paint for the stem and leaves of the flower. Paint short red lines for the petals. Without cleaning the brush, add yellow petals to the flower, allowing the colors to mix and **overlap**. Let the paint dry.

6. For added decoration, glue feathers onto the shield. String beads onto the yarn and tie each end of the string in a knot. Glue the strand onto the shield.

One Step More

Explain that legends are passed down from generation to generation through storytelling. Share some examples of legends and have children tell or write a legend of their own. Learn other facts about the Native American culture and write them on index cards or strips of construction paper.

Art Show

Mount the finished shields on larger sheets of brightly colored or black paper. Display the shields with children's written legends. Add Native American cultural facts to the display.

 Bookshelf

Arrow to the Sun: A Pueblo Indian Tale by Gerald McDermott (Penguin Putnam Books for Young Readers, 1977)

Coyote Steals the Blanket: A Ute Tale by Janet Stevens (Holiday House, 1994)

Coyote: A Trickster Tale From the American Southwest by Gerald McDermott (Harcourt, 1999)

The Legend of the Bluebonnet by Tomie dePaola (Penguin Putnam Books for Young Readers, 1996)

The Legend of the Indian Paintbrush by Tomie dePaola (Putnam, 1988)

New Art Words

express
cartoonlike
portrait
tint

Materials

* mood chart (see page 36)
* 9- by 12-inch white paper
* crayons
* tempera paint (white and various colors)
* paintbrushes
* water containers
* paper plates
* scissors
* 9- by 12-inch colored paper to match paint colors
* glue
* sample paint charts (optional; available at paint stores)
* black paper (for mounting)

My Many Colored Days

by Dr. Seuss
illustrated by Steve Johnson and Lou Fancher

Children paint an expressive portrait—using a specific color to illustrate a certain mood.

Let's Begin

Read aloud *My Many Colored Days* to the class. This book is a terrific tool to encourage discussion about how emotions and colors are linked and how colors can **express** moods. Ask children to close their eyes and imagine themselves surrounded by a particular color (for example, blue). Ask: "What feelings or moods come to mind?" (Typical responses to blue might include peaceful, calm, lonely, relaxed, and happy.) Invite children to picture what feeling like a certain color might look like. Ask: "What images do you see?" (Some responses to blue might include the sky, water, and someone napping.)

Make enlarged copies of the mood chart on page 36.
Color each face the appropriate color. Cover work
surfaces to prepare for painting. Prepare each table with
one color of paint and matching crayons (for example,
blue paint and blue crayons). Place a container of white
paint at each painting station as well. Pass out the
materials. Then demonstrate the following procedures
as children follow along.

Step by Step

1. Show children the mood chart. Using a crayon on a
sheet of white paper, draw a large **cartoonlike** face
to illustrate the expressive quality of the color of paint
at the table. Explain that you have drawn a **portrait**.

2. Paint the facial features (eyes, nose, and mouth).

3. Show pictures from the book again, and observe how
the illustrators mixed white paint with colored paint to
create different **tints**, or shades, of color. On a paper
plate, combine white paint with colored paint to create
a lighter shade. Use a variety of tints to paint around
the facial features. Let the painting dry.

4. Cut out the face.

5. Select a sheet of paper to match the color of the
painted face. Draw a figure using simple shapes. Draw
the figure in a position that represents the mood of
the color and matches the expression of the face.

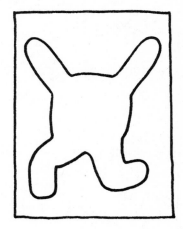

6. Cut out the figure. Glue the face onto the figure.

7. Cut strips of paper from the same color paper. To
create different styles of hair, fold or curl the strips.
Attach the hair with glue.

★ TIP Accent facial features with colored paper.

Bookshelf

Chidi Only Likes Blue: An African Book of Colours by Ifeoma Onyefulu (Cobblehill Books, 1997)

Color, Color, Color, Color by Ruth Heller (Putnam & Grosset, 1995)

A Color of His Own by Leo Lionni (Knopf, 1997)

I Feel Orange Today by Patricia Godwin (Annick Press, Limited, 1993)

My Many Colored Days by Dr. Seuss (Knopf, 1996)

Related Video

Notes Alive: Dr. Seuss's My Many Colored Days Narrated by Holly Hunter (Minnesota Orchestral Association, 1999)

One Step More

To further illustrate the concept of tints, look at color charts from paint stores that show many variations of one color. Using crayons, draw a particular place that illustrates a certain mood or feeling; be sure to use colors that contribute to that feeling.

Art Show

To emphasize color, cover a bulletin board with black paper and display the figures on it. (Or mount the projects individually on sheets of black paper.) Copy quotations from the book onto large sheets of paper and add them to the display. This will help demonstrate the connection between colors and emotions. Attach a paint store sample to each project to illustrate the tints of color used.

gray—frustrated  blue—sad  orange—excited

pink—content  yellow—happy  purple—worried

green—nervous  red—angry  white—surprised

Chicka Chicka Boom Boom

**by Bill Martin Jr. and
John Archambault
illustrated by Lois Ehlert**

*Working in a cooperative group,
children illustrate the alphabet
with block letters on brightly
colored paper.*

New Art Words

border
collaboration
block letter

Let's Begin

Read aloud *Chicka Chicka Boom Boom* to
the class. Look closely at the alphabet
letters and **border** designs in the book.
Explain that this project is a cooperative
one—a **collaboration** in which the
class will work together to complete
one finished piece of artwork. Ask:
"What are the benefits of working
together on a project? What are some
problems we might encounter? What
are some ways we can avoid or solve
these problems?"

 ## Materials

* large sheet of white craft
  paper
* large sheet of brown craft
  paper
* 4- by 4-inch colored paper
* pencils
* letter templates (optional,
  pages 40–41)
* scissors
* 9- by 12-inch red, green, and
  brown paper
* 6- by 12-inch pink paper
* glue

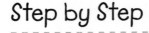

In advance, cut out a large tree trunk from brown craft paper and glue it onto the white craft paper. The trunk should be several feet long. Cut the red paper in half vertically so that it measures 4 1/2 by 12 inches.

Pass out the materials. Then demonstrate the following procedures as children follow along.

Step by Step

1. Demonstrate how to draw a simple **block letter**. Children can use the book as a reference, or you can distribute enlarged copies of the letter templates.

2. Give each child a sheet of 4- by 4-inch paper, alternating colors as you distribute the paper. While passing out the paper, assign each child a different letter to draw.

3. Have children draw or trace their letters and cut them out.

4. Cut a few coconuts from brown paper and palm tree leaves from green paper. Glue these onto the tree trunk.

5. Create a border with the red paper. Then cut circles from the pink paper and glue them onto the border for decoration.

6. As children recite the alphabet, have them glue their letter in order onto the tree.

One Step More

Make a collage with alphabet letters found in magazines or newspapers. Or have children create individual projects by drawing the Chicka Chicka Boom Boom tree with crayons on construction paper—good practice for writing the entire alphabet!

Art Show

Display the group mural with the book title. Children can also present their mural to another class or to other teachers as they recite or sing the ABC's.

 Bookshelf

An Aardvark Flew an Airplane . . . and Other Silly Alphabet Rhymes by David Dadson (Little Thinker Books, 2000)

The Alphabet Tree by Leo Lionni (Knopf, 1990)

Chicka Chicka Boom Boom by Bill Martin, Jr. and John Archambault (Simon & Schuster Books for Young Readers, 1989)

Once Upon A–Z: An Alphabet Odyssey by Jodi Linscott (Doubleday, 1991)

26 Letters and 99 Cents by Tana Hoban (Greenwillow Books, 1987)

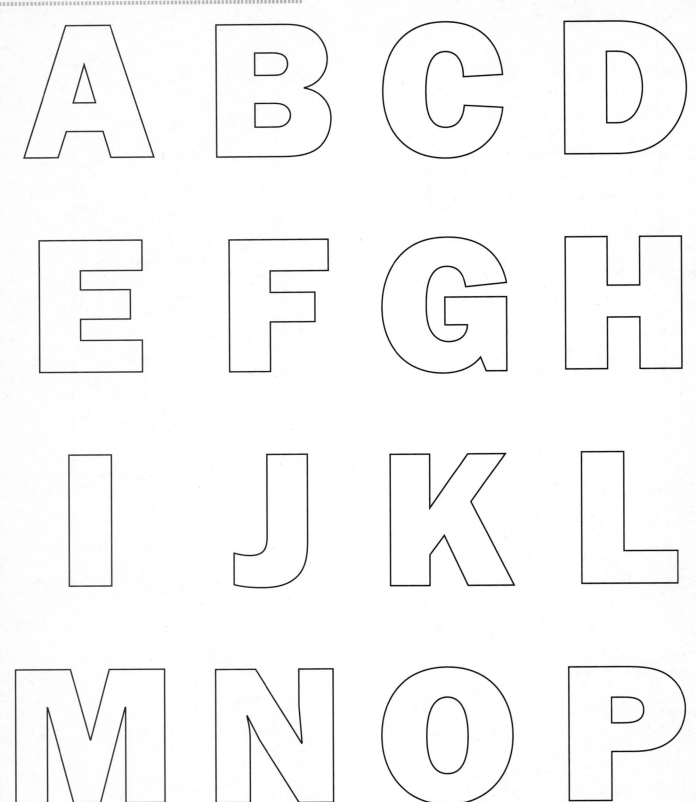

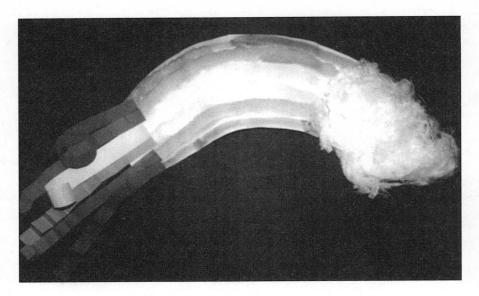

New Art Words

spectrum
blend
accordion fold

Materials

* pictures of rainbows
* 12- by 18-inch white drawing paper
* watercolor paints
* watercolor brushes
* water containers
* scissors
* 1- by 12-inch paper strips in the colors of the spectrum (red, orange, yellow, green, blue, indigo, violet)
* glue
* cotton or polyester batting

Color Dance

by Ann Jonas

Children learn about the color spectrum as they paint a watercolor rainbow with a decorative twist.

Let's Begin

Read aloud *Color Dance* to the class. The end of the story shows the colors in a circle, as in a rainbow **spectrum**. Show children pictures of rainbows. Ask: "Are the colors of the rainbow in a specific order? Where have you seen rainbows before? Have you ever seen a rainbow in a puddle or a lawn sprinkler?"

To help children remember the colors of the spectrum, discuss the acronym ROY G. BIV (red, orange, yellow, green, blue, indigo, violet). Note that indigo is in the spectrum but is not always included in rainbow pictures.

Cover work surfaces to prepare for painting, and pass out the materials. Then demonstrate the following procedures as children follow along.

Step by Step

1. Begin by painting a red curved line for the top of the rainbow. The band should be approximately one inch thick. Discuss how the watercolors, because they are wet, will **blend** together as you paint. Make sure each color touches the previous color.

 **TIP** If students need help with this project, draw a curved line on the top section of each paper, as a guide for the rainbow painting.

2. Continue the progression of colors, making wide paint strokes in the curved shape. Wash the brushes between each color. Let the painting dry.

 **TIP** Explain to children that watercolors are set up in spectrum order in the palette.

3. Cut out the painted rainbow.

4. Distribute the colored strips of paper, making sure each child gets one strip of each color. Demonstrate how the papers may be curled or **accordian folded**. Explain that these will decorate the end of the rainbow.

5. Glue the strips of paper to each matching color at one end of the rainbow.

6. Glue a cotton or polyester batting cloud to the other end of the rainbow.

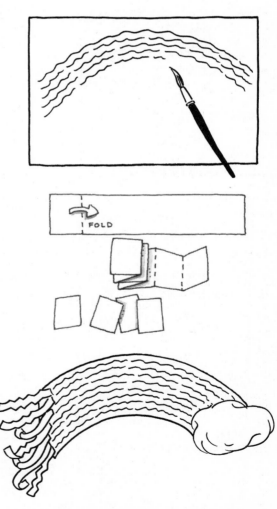

Bookshelf

***Afro-Bets Book of Colors:
Meet the Color Family*** by
Margery Brown (Just Us
Books, 2000)

***The Black & White
Rainbow*** by John Trent
(Waterbrook Press, 1999)

Color Dance by Ann Jonas
(Greenwillow Books, 1989)

***The Day the Rainbow Lost
Its Color*** by Jon Butler
(Staircase Publishing, 1997)

My Box of Color by
Lorianne Siomades (Boyds
Mills Press, 1998)

Rainbow Joe & Me by
Maria Diaz Strom (Lee &
Low Books, 1999)

A Rainbow of Friends by
P. K. Hallinan (Ideals Children's
Books, 1994)

One Step More

Combine this art project with a science lesson by
experimenting with prisms. A prism illustrates how
light splits into colors. Raindrops act as prisms. Ask:
"Other than in the sky, where else have you seen a
rainbow?" Many children will have seen the prism effect
in puddles, a hose spray, or a waterfall spray.

Art Show

Display the paintings over classroom doors in the hallway
or on a bulletin board with a blue paper background. On
a separate sheet of paper, have children write the acronym
ROY G. BIV using the colors of the spectrum (for example,
write *R* with a red crayon, and so on). Attach the papers to
their rainbow paintings.

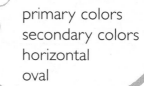

New Art Words

primary colors
secondary colors
horizontal
oval

Mouse Paint

by Ellen Walsh Stoll

*Children mix paint to turn primary colors
into secondary colors—and create adorable,
colorful mice!*

Let's Begin

Read aloud *Mouse Paint* to the class. This amusing
tale is a great introduction to the concept of mixing
colors to create new ones. Children will find out for
themselves what happens when pairs of **primary
colors** (red, yellow, and blue) are combined.

The new colors made by mixing two primary colors
are called **secondary colors**. Red + blue = purple;
blue + yellow = green; red + yellow = orange. Ask
why "secondary color" is a good name for these colors.

Cover work surfaces to prepare for painting, and pass
out the materials. Use paper or foam plates as paint
palettes. Then demonstrate the following procedures
as children follow along.

Materials

* pencils
* 10- by 16-inch white paper
* tempera paint (red, yellow, blue, black, and white)
* paper or foam plates
* paintbrushes (various sizes)
* water containers
* 1- by 4-inch pieces of cardboard
* construction paper scraps (red, yellow, blue, green, purple, and orange)
* glue
* black crayons
* white paper strips (optional)
* colored paper (optional, for mounting)

Step by Step

1. Place a sheet of white paper in a **horizontal** position. Use a pencil to draw three **ovals**. Tell children to make each oval approximately the same size as their hand.

2. Begin with one pair of colors. Paint an oval using one of the colors. Working quickly so the paint stays wet, use a clean brush to add the second color. With a third clean brush, gently stir the colors on the oval to make the new secondary color.

TIP

To prevent the unwanted mixing of colors, leave each paintbrush in its designated paint container. Use a clean, separate paintbrush to do the mixing.

3. While the paint is wet, paint two short lines for arms. Use the brush to make ears in the shape of ovals and feet in the shape of the letter *L*.

4. Paint each mouse using a different pair of colors in the same way. The three mice should be purple, green, and orange. Let the paintings dry.

5. With white tempera paint and a thin brush, make two eyes for each mouse.

6. Use the black tempera paint to make a small dot for the nose. Paint fingers, toes, and the insides of the ears. Dip the short end of a cardboard piece into the paint and print the whiskers. Then print several lines in a row for the tail.

7. From the paper scraps, tear two small pieces of red, yellow, and blue construction paper. Match the two primary colors that were mixed to create the color of each mouse. Glue the two pieces beneath each mouse along with a piece of paper that is the same color as the mouse. For example, glue red, yellow, and orange pieces under the orange mouse.

One Step More

Write recipes for mixing the primary colors to create secondary colors (red + yellow = orange, and so on). Glue scraps of the appropriate colored paper above each word. Explore color mixing further by combining water tinted with food coloring, or by looking at the world through a pair of colored glasses (for example, see what the sky looks like through a pair of yellow-tinted sunglasses).

Art Show

Mount the finished projects on one or more larger sheets of colored paper. Display the recipes beneath the mouse paintings. Study a color wheel and add it to the display.

Bookshelf

Color Dance by Ann Jonas (HarperCollins Children's Book Group, 1989)

A Color of His Own by Leo Lionni (Knopf, 2001)

Little Blue & Little Yellow by Leo Lionni (Astor-Honor, Inc., 1959)

Mouse Paint by Ellen Walsh Stoll (Harcourt, 1989)

My Box of Color by Lorianne Siomades (Boyds Mills Press, 1998)

New Art Words

contrast
vertical
texture

 ## Materials

- ✴ pictures of sunflowers, real or artificial sunflowers
- ✴ 12- by 18-inch construction paper (blue, red, or purple)
- ✴ tempera paint (yellow, orange, and green)
- ✴ large paintbrushes
- ✴ water containers
- ✴ black or brown burlap
- ✴ scissors
- ✴ glue
- ✴ real sunflower seeds or white chalk
- ✴ white or light-colored paper (optional, for mounting)

 ## TIP

If you are working with very young children, or if time is short, burlap circles may be cut out ahead of time. The diameters should measure about 2 inches.

Camille and the Sunflowers: A Story About Vincent van Gogh

by Laurence Anholt

Children use tempera paint and burlap to create their own version of a textured sunflower garden.

Let's Begin

Read aloud *Camille and the Sunflowers: A Story About Vincent van Gogh* to the class. Observe what a real sunflower looks like (use photographs or a real or artificial sunflower). Ask: "What is your first impression of the sunflower? Do van Gogh's sunflowers look different from the real thing? How? Was van Gogh trying to copy exactly what a sunflower looks like?" Notice van Gogh's use of

Activity continued on page 49.

Papa, Please Get the Moon for Me
by Eric Carle
page 7

There Was an Old Lady Who Swallowed a Fly
by Simms Taback
page 9

Tar Beach
by Faith Ringgold
page 12

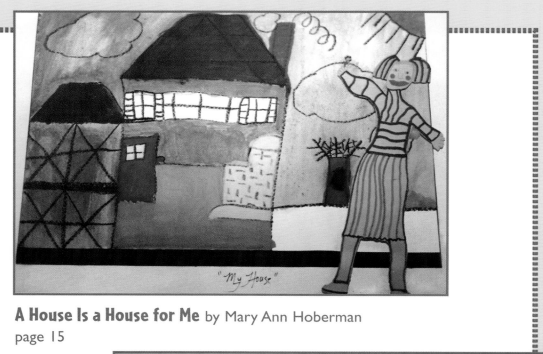

A House Is a House for Me by Mary Ann Hoberman
page 15

In the Small, Small Pond
by Denise Fleming
page 17

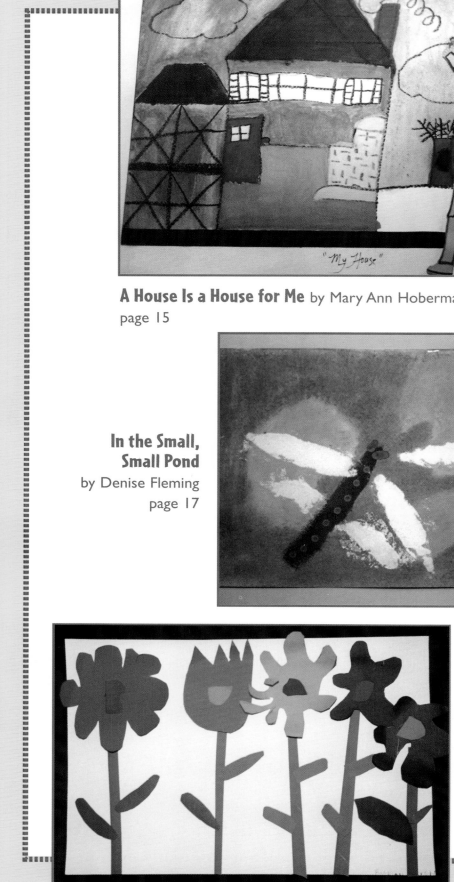

Planting a Rainbow
by Lois Ehlert
page 20

I like to make snowballs.

**My Many
Colored Days**
by Dr. Seuss
page 34

**The Legend of the
Indian Paintbrush**
by Tomie dePaola
page 31

Chicka Chicka Boom Boom
by Bill Martin Jr. and John Archambault
page 37

Color Dance
by Ann Jonas
page 42

Camille and the Sunflowers: A Story About Vincent van Gogh
by Laurence Anholt
page 48

Heather and the red marker

Harold and the Purple Crayon
by Crockett Johnson
page 51

yellow + red = orange

blue + yellow = green

red + blue = purple

Mouse Paint
by Ellen Stoll Walsh
page 45

Matthew's Dream by Leo Lionni
page 54

Swimmy by Leo Lionni
page 57

Corduroy
by Don Freeman
page 59

Cat's Colors
by Jane Cabrera
page 63

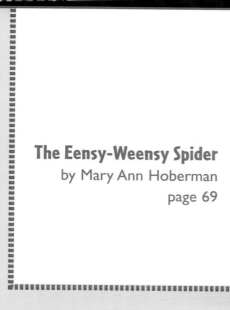

Owl Moon
by Jane Yolen
page 66

The Eensy-Weensy Spider
by Mary Ann Hoberman
page 69

Elmer
by David McKee
page 72

Huggly Takes a Bath
by Tedd Arnold
page 75

**The Little Engine
That Could**
by Watty Piper
page 78

bright colors and movement in his paintings. These elements of his style are well illustrated in the book.

Cover work surfaces to prepare for painting and pass out the materials. Then demonstrate the following procedures as children follow along.

Step by Step

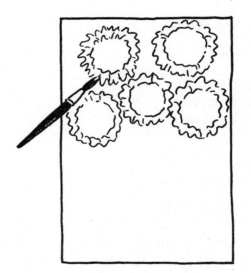

1. Choose a sheet of colored construction paper. Explain that the dark color will create a nice **contrast** with the yellow sunflowers. Place the paper in a **vertical** position.

2. Using yellow and orange paint, paint three to five circles of flower petals near the top of the paper. Use both colors to create cheerful sunflowers. Be sure to leave the centers unpainted; this is where the burlap will be placed.

3. Use the green paint to paint long stems from the flowers to the bottom of the paper. Paint several leaves on each stem. Allow the painting to dry.

4. While the painting dries, cut circles of burlap to fit inside the center of each sunflower. The burlap will add **texture** to the painting.

5. After the painting is dry, glue a burlap circle to the center of each flower.

6. Use the white chalk to add seeds to the burlap, or glue real sunflower seeds to the burlap.

Bookshelf

Backyard Sunflower by Elizabeth King (Penguin Putnam Books for Young Readers, 1993)

Camille and the Sunflowers: A Story About Vincent van Gogh by Laurence Anholt (Barron's Educational Series, 1994)

A Handful of Sunshine: Growing a Sunflower by Melanie Eclare (Ragged Bear, 2000)

The Starry Night by Neil Waldman (Boyds Mills Press, 1999)

Sunflowers by Gail Saunders-Smith (Pebble Books, 2000)

Van Gogh by Mike Venezia (Children's Press, 1988)

Van Gogh: Famous Artist by Andrew S. Hughes (Barron's Educational Series, 1994)

One Step More

Plant sunflower seeds in the classroom or on the school grounds in the spring. Show and discuss other examples of van Gogh's work.

Art Show

Mount the finished painting on larger sheets of white or light-colored paper. Display the paintings along with pictures of sunflowers or real sunflowers. You might also add reproductions of van Gogh's sunflower paintings.

Heather and the red marker

Harold and the Purple Crayon

by Crockett Johnson

Children use their imagination to take a journey and create a continuous line drawing. To tell a story, all you need are markers and paper!

Let's Begin

Read aloud *Harold and the Purple Crayon* to the class. Harold illustrates an adventure using his favorite purple crayon. Explain that Harold's story is an example of the power of imagination. Harold finds a solution when he encounters a problem in his pictures. Discuss the problems Harold has and how he solves them. (For example, he gets into a scary situation when he draws a monster in his picture.) Ask children if they have ever come up with a good solution to a problem.

New Art Words

continuous line
drawing
horizontal
overlap

 ## Materials

* photographs of sailboats
* 9- by 12-inch white paper
* colored markers
* white paper strips (optional)
* black paper (optional, for mounting)

Notice that Crockett Johnson's illustrations are very simple. He uses just one line to show Harold's purple crayon traveling over the sea, across the sky, and back to his room through the pages of the book. Explain to children that they will create a drawing using only one color and one connecting line. Artists call this a **continuous line drawing**. This style is often used to strengthen observational skills.

Pass out the materials. Then demonstrate the following procedures as children follow along.

Step by Step

1. Observe the photographs of sailboats and discuss what children might see if they were sailing in a boat. Place the paper in a **horizontal** position.

2. Show children how to draw the sea and a sailboat using only one line, first with your finger and then with a marker. Make a game out of trying not to pick up the marker as you draw. It's not so hard to do—it just takes practice!

 **TIP**

Children may feel more comfortable if you make a mistake and pick up your marker. Then show that you can begin again where you left off.

3. Guide children in planning their drawing. Have them first practice drawing with just their finger. Then have them select a favorite color marker. Remind children to try not to pick up their marker as they draw. If they forget, they can put the marker back at the spot where it was picked up. Explain that lines may **overlap**. Continuous line drawing requires concentration!

One Step More

Choose an object to draw (such as a flower or a tool). Create a continuous line drawing without looking at the drawing and without picking up your pencil. Explain to children that their eyes should follow along the outer edge of the object as their hand is drawing it. Artists often do this exercise to improve their observational skills. Children love this challenge—it's harder to keep their eyes off the paper than they would expect!

Art Show

Display the drawings with photographs of sailboats. Use each child's name and marker color for a title, such as "Jessica and the Blue Marker." Mount the drawings with the titles on larger sheets of black paper.

Bookshelf

Harold and the Purple Crayon by Crockett Johnson (Harper & Row, 1955)

Harold's Circus by Crockett Johnson (HarperCollins, 1981)

Harold's Trip to the Sky by Crockett Johnson (HarperCollins, 1981)

It's Funny Where Ben's Train Takes Him by Robert Burleigh (Scholastic, 1999)

My Crayons Talk by Patricia Hubbard (Holt, 1999)

The Trip by Ezra Jack Keats (Morrow/Avon, 1987)

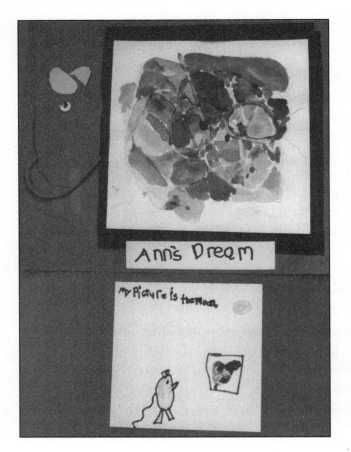

Materials

- 9- by 9-inch white paper
- crayons
- watercolor paints
- small paintbrushes
- water containers
- glue
- 12- by 18-inch construction paper (various colors)
- 10- by 1-inch strips of black paper
- 6- by 6-inch gray paper
- scraps of colored paper
- scissors
- moveable eyes
- yarn
- 1- by 4-inch strips of white paper
- 6- by 6-inch white paper
- markers
- colored paper (optional, for mounting)

Matthew's Dream

by Leo Lionni

Children create abstract art using crayons, construction paper, and watercolor paints.

Let's Begin

Read aloud *Matthew's Dream* to the class. Ask: "Why did Matthew want to become an artist?" Explain that artists work in many different ways. Every artist seeks to create works of art that are **unique**, or one of a kind, to express his or her ideas, dreams, and feelings. Ask: "What are some ways that artists express themselves? How do you like to express yourself?"

Look at other works by abstract artists and talk about the feelings, emotions, or ideas that are represented. For example, how does Jackson Pollock's splatter-painted art make you feel? How does a Mark Rothko color-block painting make you feel?

Cover work surfaces to prepare for painting, and pass out the materials. Then demonstrate the following procedures as children follow along.

Step by Step

1. Place a sheet of white paper in front of you. As children watch, select a crayon, close your eyes, and begin drawing several swirling lines on the paper. Create loosely interwoven lines. (If the lines are too close together, the project will be difficult. Demonstrate how to move your hand across the page to ensure that the lines are spread out.) If you go off the paper, it is okay. Count slowly to ten as you draw and then stop and open your eyes.

2. Look carefully at the drawing. Does the drawing look like anything in particular? This type of drawing, which does not represent a realistic picture, is an example of **abstract** art. Ask: "What shapes do you see in this drawing?" Find shapes that make you think of certain images, such as a cloud, a rock, or an elephant's ear. Have children close their eyes and do their own crayon drawings while you count to ten.

3. Use watercolors to paint the shapes in between the lines. Switch colors often. Encourage children to use different paint colors for shapes that are touching. Let the painting dry.

4. Glue the painting onto the right side of a sheet of 12- by 18-inch colored paper.

Bookshelf

The Art Lesson by Tomie dePaola (Penguin Putnam Books for Young Readers, 1997)

Little Cloud by Eric Carle (Penguin Putnam Books for Young Readers, 2001)

Matthew's Dream by Leo Lionni (Dragonfly Books, 1991)

Picasso: A Day in His Studio by Veronique Antoine (Chelsea House, 1994)

Picasso for Kids by Margaret Hyde (Budding Artists, 1996)

Ann's Dream

My picture is full of color.

5. To make the frame, place glue along one edge of the painting and press a strip of black paper on top. Attach strips to each side of the painting.

6. To make the mouse, draw an oval shape on the gray paper. Cut it out. Cut out ovals from colored paper for ears. Glue one ear on the front of the oval and one on the back.

7. Glue on one moveable eye.

8. Cut a small *V* shape from the mouse for the mouth.

9. Cut two legs from the paper scraps. Glue one on the back of the mouse and one on the front.

10. Glue the mouse beside the painting so that it looks like the mouse is looking at the painting. Glue yarn on the back of the mouse for a tail.

11. Write a title on a white paper strip. Instead of Matthew's Dream, include the child's name in the title (for example, "Julie's Dream"). Glue the label under the painting.

One Step More

On the 6- by 6-inch white paper, have children write a sentence or two about their dream picture. They can use this sentence starter: *My picture is . . .* Then have them use markers to draw a picture of their mouse and painting.

Art Show

Mount each child's mouse collage and explanation on a large sheet of colored paper. Create a sign with the title "Inspiration Corner." Add reproductions of abstract art to the display.

Swimmy
by Leo Lionni

In this delightful project, children create texture using tissue paper, cut paper, and salt on watercolor paints.

Let's Begin

Read aloud *Swimmy* to the class. Talk about the artistic style of author-illustrator Leo Lionni. Discuss the use of **texture** in the illustrations and, in particular, the texture of the watercolor in the background. Explain to children that they will use salt on wet paper to create a similar texture in their own projects.

Pass out the materials. Then demonstrate the following procedures as children follow along. If desired, play the audiocassette of ocean music as children work on their projects.

Step by Step

1. Tear the tissue paper into long strips. Explain that the strips will be used for sea grass. Place the strips in a pile where children can easily reach them.

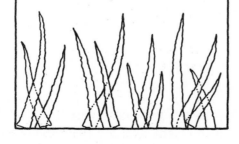

2. Place a sheet of white paper in a **horizontal** position. Using an easel brush, cover a small area of the white paper with the glue mixture. Press a strip of tissue

Materials

* tissue paper (various shades of blue, green, and purple)
* 12- by 18-inch white construction paper
* easel brushes
* a mixture of white glue and water (in equal parts)
* paintbrushes
* water containers
* watercolor paints
* salt (canning or regular)
* 9- by 2-inch construction paper strips (orange, yellow, and red)
* pencils
* scissors
* glue
* black markers or crayons
* audiocassette of ocean music (optional)

paper in a **vertical** position onto the glued area. Lightly brush the edges of the tissue with the glue mixture to secure it to the construction paper. Glue several more tissue paper strips onto the paper in the same way. Be sure to leave white space around the strips.

3. Dip a paintbrush in water and wet the areas around the strips of tissue. With a paintbrush, apply blue and green watercolor paint to the wet areas. While the paper is wet, sprinkle it with salt. The salt will absorb the water and create texture. Allow the paint to dry.

4. Choose a construction paper strip and fold it in half lengthwise. Then fold it in half lengthwise again. With a pencil, draw a fish on the folded paper so that it fills the space. Keeping the paper folded, cut out the fish. In this way, you will cut four fish at the same time. Choose a paper strip of a different color and make four more fish.

5. Ask children if they know what a school of fish is. Show them an illustration of a school of fish in the story. Glue the fish onto the water scene so that they form a school. With a black marker or crayon, add an eye to each fish. If desired, add scales or gills.

Bookshelf

A Color of His Own by Leo Lionni (Pantheon, 1975)

Fish Is Fish by Leo Lionni (Pantheon, 1970)

Frank the Fish Gets His Wish by Laura Appleton-Smith (Flyleaf Publishing, 1998)

The Rainbow Fish by Marcus Pfister (North-South Books, 1992)

Rainbow Fish to the Rescue! by Marcus Pfister (North-South Books, 1995)

Swimmy by Leo Lionni (Knopf, 1973)

One Step More

Read *The Rainbow Fish* by Marcus Pfister, and create a similar project following the same procedures. To make a rainbow fish like the one in Pfister's book, add iridescent scales made of aluminum foil.

Art Show

Tear large pieces of craft paper to resemble seaweed. Attach the giant seaweed to a bulletin board along with the finished projects to create an ocean display.

Corduroy

by Don Freeman

Construct Corduroy the bear using torn paper and corrugated cardboard—a great introduction to texture!

Let's Begin

Read aloud *Corduroy* to the class. Be sure to notice Corduroy's clothing and the missing button on his green pants. Discuss the word **texture** with the class. How does corduroy material feel? What do other materials feel like? How does a bear's fur feel? Explain that children will use **crimped** and torn paper to represent the soft, furry textures of Corduroy the bear.

New Art Words

texture
crimped
overlap

Materials

* 9- by 12-inch oaktag or heavy paper
* teddy bear template (page 62, optional)
* pencils
* scissors
* construction paper in various shades of brown
* glue
* 3- by 7-inch green construction paper
* paper crimper (or corrugated cardboard and green crayons)
* buttons
* black crayon or marker

Make enough copies of the template for children to share, and cut out the templates. Pass out the materials and then demonstrate the following procedures as children follow along.

 **TIP**

Check with your librarian to see if the school owns the stuffed Corduroy bear that accompanies this popular story.

Step by Step

1. Trace the bear pattern onto the oaktag. Cut out the bear. Or draw an outline of a bear that fills the page, and then cut it out.

2. Tear the brown construction paper into pieces about the size of a large postage stamp.

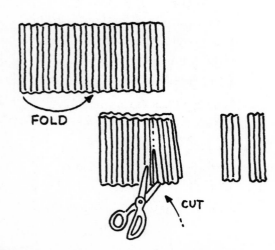

3. Glue the torn paper onto the bear so that the pieces **overlap** slightly. This will create a texture that resembles fur. Cover the entire bear with torn paper so that the oaktag is no longer visible. Allow the glue to dry.

4. Supervise children as they use the paper crimper to create the corduroy material. Crimp the green paper in one piece. (If a crimper is not available, place a piece of green paper on a piece of corrugated cardboard. Rub the paper with the side of a green crayon over the corrugated cardboard.)

 **TIP**

Real corduroy material may be used instead of crimped paper.

5. Fold the crimped paper in half and cut a one-inch piece from the open end for the overall straps.

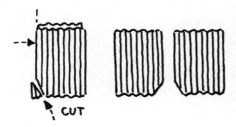

CUT

6. At the folded edge of the paper, cut off the corner. Then cut the paper along the fold. These two pieces are Corduroy's pant legs.

7. Placing the cut corner toward the center of the bear, glue the pant legs into place. Then glue the overall straps into place. (To match the story, children may want to use only one strap.)

8. Glue a button to one strap.

9. Use a black crayon or marker to add details to the face and fur.

One Step More

Have children bring in their favorite bears from home and have a teddy bear picnic! To further illustrate the concept of texture, place several objects with different textures into a shoebox with a lid (for example, a piece of felt, sandpaper, tree bark, carpet, a quarter, and a balloon). Cut a hole in the lid or side of the box. Have children feel the objects and guess what they are, based only on texture. As an alternative, you could place one object in the box at a time.

Art Show

Display the Corduroy art project in the library along with teddy bears and a copy of the book *Corduroy*.

Bookshelf

Bear by John Schoenherr (Philomel Books, 1991)

A Bear for All Seasons by Diane Marcial Fuchs (Holt, 1995)

The Berenstain Bears series by Jan and Stan Berenstain (Random House and Western Publishing Company)

Corduroy by Don Freeman (Viking Press, 1968)

Paddington Bear by Michael Bond (HarperCollins Publishers, 1998)

A Pocket for Corduroy by Don Freeman (Viking Press, 1978)

Ragged Bear by Brigitte Weninger (North-South Books, 1996)

25 Terrific Art Projects Based on Favorite Picture Books
Scholastic Professional Books

Cat's Colors

by Jane Cabrera

Children experiment with brush strokes to create the illusion of movement in a colorful painting of a cat.

Let's Begin

Read aloud *Cat's Colors* to the class. Enjoy the colorful and expressive paintings illustrated in the book. Ask: "Even though an illustration does not really move, is there a way for an artist to suggest **movement**?" The short heavy brush strokes imitate the cat's playful movement, giving the cat a sense of energy and action. The cat chooses the color orange because it reflects the image of its mother. Ask: "What is your favorite color? Why?"

Cover work surfaces to prepare for painting, and pass out the materials. Then demonstrate the following procedures as children follow along.

New Art Words

movement
horizontal
pattern

 ## Materials

* 12- by 18-inch orange paper
* pencils
* tempera paints (yellow, orange, black, blue, white, and green)
* paintbrushes
* water containers
* scissors
* 12- by 18-inch white paper
* glue

Step by Step

1. Place a sheet of orange paper in a **horizontal** position. Draw simple shapes for the body parts of a cat: a large circle for the head, an oval for the body, a snake shape for the tail, and rectangles for the legs.

2. Use small brush strokes to paint the cat's fur yellow and orange. The strokes indicate the **pattern** of fur. Allow some orange paper to show through.

3. Use black paint to outline the eyes, ears, whiskers, mouth, claws, and stripes. Allow the paint to dry.

4. Cut out the cat.

TIP

To avoid cutting off the tail or legs, some children may need assistance drawing a crayon outline around the cat before cutting.

5. Place the white paper in a horizontal position. Cover the top three-quarters of the paper with blue and white paint for the sky. Demonstrate that painting short, varied brush strokes in different directions will help to create an illusion of movement in the sky.

6. Use upward and downward brush strokes to paint a grassy edge along the bottom of the page. Let the yellow, blue, and green paints mix directly on the paper to create a multicolored ground. Allow the paint to dry.

7. Glue the cat onto the painting so that it looks as if it is walking through the grass.

One Step More

Choose a favorite color. Paint another picture using only that color. Experiment by adding white or black to the color to create highlights and shadows.

Art Show

Display the artwork on brightly colored background paper along with pictures of tiger cats. Make a graph depicting students' favorite colors. Display the graph along with their artwork.

Bookshelf

Cat's Colors by Jane Cabrera (Penguin Putnam Books for Young Readers, 2000)

The Crayon Box That Talked by Shane DeRolf (Random House, 1997)

I Feel Orange Today by Patricia Godwin (Annick Press, Limited, 1993)

Top Cat by Lois Ehlert (Harcourt Children's Books, 2001)

When Cats Dream by Dav Pilkey (Orchard Books, 1992)

New Art Words

crayon resist
tempera paint wash
focal point

Materials

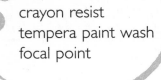

- ✱ 12- by 18-inch drawing paper
- ✱ pencils
- ✱ brown and black crayons
- ✱ watercolor paints
- ✱ watercolor brushes
- ✱ water containers
- ✱ blue and black tempera paints, thinned with water
- ✱ wide foam brushes or sponges
- ✱ scraps of green construction paper (optional)
- ✱ black construction paper (optional, for mounting)

Owl Moon

by Jane Yolen

illustrated by John Schoenherr

Soft watercolor illustrations in this story inspire a crayon-resist painting of an owl in the night.

Let's Begin

Read aloud *Owl Moon* to the class. The beautiful watercolor illustrations in this story enhance the poetic manner in which the story of "owling" is told. Ask: "Why are watercolors a good medium with which to illustrate this story?"

Explain to students that they will create their own portrait of an owl using a technique called **crayon resist**. This technique involves painting watercolors over a crayon drawing. The wax from the crayons resists the water in the watercolor paint so that both the crayons and the watercolor appear on the page together. A **tempera paint wash**, paint diluted with water, will complete the sky area.

Cover work surfaces to prepare for painting, and pass out the materials. Then demonstrate the following procedures as children follow along.

TIP Make the blue and black tempera washes ahead of time. Mix about one tablespoon of paint with approximately 2 cups of water. Make a separate wash for each color.

Step by Step

1. Using a pencil, draw a wide tree branch as a perch for the owl. Draw the branch all the way across the bottom of the paper.

2. Demonstrate how to draw an owl, as shown.

TIP Draw a figure eight for the body, then add wings that slope downward.

3. Draw the owl's eyes and beak with the black crayon.

4. Heavily trace over the drawing with the black and brown crayons. Add texture to the body, wings, and branch by using a variety of lines.

5. To paint the owl, wet the brush and use only a little paint. Yellows and browns may be combined for the owl colors. In the crayon-resist technique, the wax of the crayon will repel the paint and remain visible.

TIP Leave small areas on the bird unpainted to add more texture to the feathers.

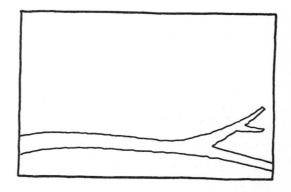

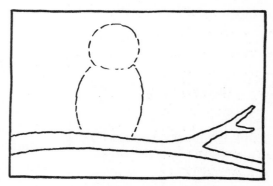

6. Use an almost dry brush to apply paint to the facial features. Explain that too much water will make the colors run together.

7. Paint the tree branch using brown and black watercolors.

8. Paint the sky with diluted black and blue tempera paint. Dip a foam brush into the paint and press it against the edge of the container to squeeze out excess paint. The sky area should create a smooth, muted effect, making the owl the **focal point** of the artwork. Drag the brush across the page to paint the sky area. Be careful not to touch the owl or branch with the brush. Let the painting dry.

 **TIP**

Set up a work station with several containers of the diluted blue and black tempera paint wash along with foam brushes or sponges. As children finish their watercolor paintings, instruct them to come to the tempera paint work station to complete the sky. Stir the tempera mixture during the watercolor painting process.

 **Bookshelf**

The Frightened Little Owl by Mark Ezra (Interlink Publishing Group, 1997)

Owl Babies by Martin Waddell (Candlewick Press, 1992)

Owl at Home by Arnold Lobel (HarperTrophy, 1996)

Owl Moon by Jane Yolen (Philomel, 1987)

Welcome to the World of Owls by Diane Swanson (Turtleback Books, 1997)

One Step More

After the painting has dried, add cut paper leaves to create a collage. Combine this art project with a science lesson by studying more about owls and their habitat and lifestyle. Children will enjoy pretending they are "owling" by making soft "*who-o-o-o*" sounds.

Art Show

Mount the artwork on black paper. Display the owls on a large tree branch, along with pictures of real owls and the letters "WHO-O-O-O." Have children share some owl facts they have learned from the book and from further study. Write the owl facts on strips of construction paper and add them to the display.

New Art Words

radial design
diagonal

The Eensy-Weensy Spider

by Mary Ann Hoberman

illustrated by Nadine Bernard Westcott

Children sculpt a three-dimensional spider using salt dough and create a spiderweb using a radial design.

Let's Begin

Read aloud *The Eensy-Weensy Spider* to the class. Observe pictures of real spiderwebs and discuss how spiders create their webs. A spiderweb is an example of a **radial design** found in nature. A radial design begins in the middle and radiates out from that point; a spider begins weaving its web from the center and radiates out from that point. Can you think of any other examples of radial designs? Radial designs can also be found in seashells, cut halves of oranges and lemons, and snowflakes. The spokes of a bicycle are a machine-made example of a radial design.

 Materials

* photographs and drawings of spiders and spiderwebs
* 10- by 10-inch construction paper
* crayons and/or colored chalk
* squeeze bottles of glue
* glitter
* salt dough (see recipe on page 71)
* pipe cleaners in various colors (3-inches in length)
* moveable eyes
* 2-inch circles of oaktag or light cardboard

In this activity, designed for younger children, a simple spider is made from a small ball of salt dough, two moveable eyes, and eight pipe-cleaner legs. If you choose to make this activity scientifically accurate, attach two small balls of salt dough (one for the cephalothorax in the front and one for the abdomen in the back). Attach four legs to each side of the cephalothorax and eight eyes to the front.

Pass out the materials. Then demonstrate the following procedures as children follow along.

Step by Step

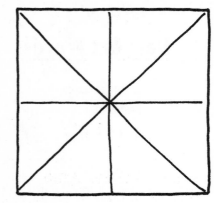

1. Select a crayon or chalk color that will show up on the construction paper. Make a small dot in the middle of the paper.

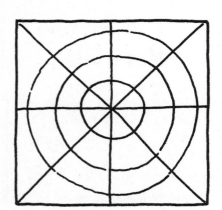

2. Draw four lines, making sure that each touches the dot in the middle of the paper. Beginning in a top corner, draw a **diagonal** line to the opposite bottom corner, touching the dot in the middle. Draw another diagonal line that runs from the opposite corner, making an *X*. Draw a line from top to bottom, and then a line from side to side.

TIP It might be helpful for younger children to "draw" imaginary lines with their fingers before using crayons or chalk.

3. Draw a circle around the dot in the middle. Leave a space and draw another circle. Continue creating a spiderweb by drawing larger and larger circles until the paper is filled.

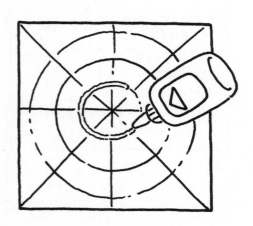

4. Squeeze a thin line of glue on top of the crayon lines.

5. Place the paper on a tray and sprinkle glitter on the web design. Shake the excess glitter onto the tray. Lay the paper flat to dry.

6. To make the spider, take a small amount of salt dough (the size of a marble) and roll it into a ball. Gently press the ball onto a table to flatten the bottom.

7. For the spider's legs, bend eight pieces of pipe cleaners. Carefully push the pipe cleaners, one at a time, into the spider's body so they are even on both sides, forming eight legs.

8. Glue two moveable eyes on top of the spider.

9. Put glue on a 2-inch circle of oaktag and place the spider on top. Let it dry. Glue the oaktag circle onto the web.

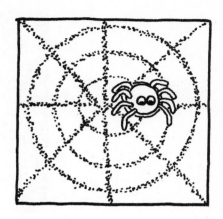

One Step More

Draw a picture using radial design. Instead of making a spiderweb, what else could you make? Radial design can also be used to create abstract art. Look through magazines to find examples of radial design.

Art Show

Make a large spiderweb using yarn on a bulletin board or large wall. Display children's spiderwebs on and around the large web. Display photographs or drawings of other examples of radial design.

Recipe: Salt Dough

2 cups table salt   1 cup cornstarch   1 ½ cups water

Stir the ingredients together in a saucepan over low heat, stirring continuously, until mixture forms a ball (about 10–15 minutes). Place dough on waxed paper. When it is cool enough to handle, knead it for three minutes. Dough can be made ahead of time and covered with foil. Knead before using. Food coloring or powdered paint may be added.

Makes approximately 30 small balls

Bookshelf

Anansi the Spider: A Tale from the Ashanti by Gerald McDermott (Henry Holt, 1972)

The Eensy-Weensy Spider by Mary Ann Hoberman (Little, Brown & Company, 2000)

The Itsy Bitsy Spider by Jeanette Winter (Harcourt Children's Books, 2000)

Nature's Paintbrush: The Patterns and Colors Around You by Susan Stockdale (Simon & Schuster, 1999)

Spiders by Gail Gibbons (Holiday House, 1994)

Spider's Lunch by Joanna Cole (Penguin Putnam Books for Young Readers, 1995)

Spiders Spin Webs by Yvonne Winer (Charlesbridge Publishing, 1996)

The Very Busy Spider by Eric Carle (Philomel Books, 1995)

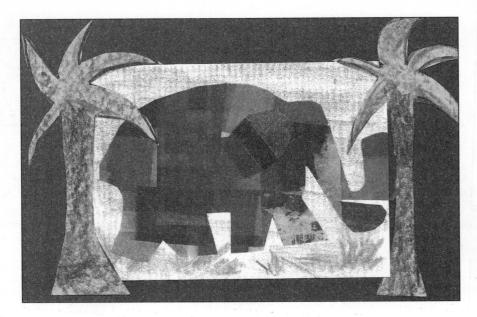

patchwork
pattern
collage

Materials

* 9- by 12-inch white paper
* mixture of white glue and water (in equal parts)
* assorted tissue paper, cut into 2-inch squares
* plastic containers
* stiff paintbrushes
* pencils
* scissors
* crayons
* 3- by 12-inch light blue paper
* 12- by 14-inch green mounting paper

Elmer
by David McKee

Children create a tissue paper collage of the colorful elephant, Elmer.

Let's Begin

Read aloud *Elmer* to the class. Ask: "What makes Elmer special?" Individuality, bright **patchwork** colors, and a sense of humor are qualities children identify with Elmer's character. Ask: "What does it mean to be a unique individual? What are some qualities that make you unique?"

Pass out the materials. Then demonstrate the following procedures as children follow along.

Step by Step

1. Paint the glue and water mixture along the edges of a sheet of white paper. Arrange the tissue paper squares in a patchwork **pattern** on top of the wet surface. The water and glue will soak through and adhere the tissue to the background. Be sure to alternate the colors. Continue painting the glue and water mixture and adding the tissue paper in rows until the paper is completely covered and all the edges have been pasted down. Explain that you have created a patchwork **collage**. Allow the glue to dry.

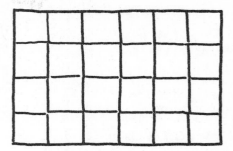

2. On the back of the tissue paper collage, fill the page with a simple outline of an elephant. (You might give younger children a template to trace.) Cut out the shape.

3. On another sheet of white paper, rub the side of an unwrapped crayon to create the sky and grass. Glue the elephant onto the middle of the paper.

 **TIP** Blue and yellow crayons combine to make rich-colored green grass.

4. On blue paper, draw simple palm trees with pointed leaves. Draw curved lines to indicate the pattern of bark. Color the trees with crayons and cut them out.

5. Mount the Elmer scene in the center of a sheet of green paper. Glue the trees onto each side to create a tropical setting.

 Bookshelf

A Bad Case of Stripes by David Shannon (Blue Sky Press, 1998)

Elmer by David McKee (HarperCollins, 1989)

Elmer Takes Off by David McKee (HarperCollins, 1998)

Elmer and Wilbur by David McKee (Lothrop, Lee & Shepard Books, 1996)

One Step More

Discuss the concept of patterns. Ask: "What other kinds of patterns can you think of besides patchwork?" Draw another picture of Elmer, and this time decorate him with other imaginative patterns. Change the scene by placing Elmer in a new setting.

Art Show

Cut out a large palm tree from colored craft paper. Display the Elmer projects all around it. Twist paper vines around the colorful elephants to create a jungle backdrop.

Huggly Takes a Bath

by Tedd Arnold

Children make textured paper using soap and paint to create a bathtime collage.

Let's Begin

Read aloud *Huggly Takes a Bath* to the class. Discuss the various parts of the **composition**, or arrangement, that will be created, including the main character, bathtub, and bubbles. All of these parts will be cut and glued onto a background to make a **collage**. Ask: "What is a collage? How do you think we can use real bubbles to create Huggly's bathtub scene?"

In advance, prepare several small containers of water. Add a teaspoon each of soap and blue paint to each container of water. Mix well.

 Materials

* water containers
* liquid dishwashing soap
* blue tempera paint
* straws
* 9- by 12-inch white construction paper
* 6- by 9-inch white drawing paper
* pencils
* black markers or crayons
* crayons
* scissors
* 6- by 12-inch colored construction paper
* glue
* 12- by 18-inch background paper (various colors)
* pieces of towel or other material (optional)

Cover work surfaces to prepare for painting, and pass out the materials. Then demonstrate the following procedures as children follow along.

Step by Step

1. Place the straw into the mixture and gently blow until bubbles form above the container. (Explain to students that you are blowing *out* of the straw.) Quickly place the white paper on top of the container, so the bubbles will print onto the paper. Repeat this several times, moving the paper around to fill it with bubble impressions. This process creates a **textured** bubble print. Let the bubble papers dry.

Safety Note: A teacher or another adult should blow the bubbles, remembering to blow out at all times. Children should not perform this step.

TIP Be sure to try making bubble paper on your own before demonstrating the process for children.

2. Draw a frog or another animal in pencil on a sheet of 6- by 9-inch white paper.

3. Trace over the character with a black marker or crayon. Color the character with crayons and cut it out.

4. In pencil, draw the bathtub on a sheet of 6- by 12-inch colored paper. First draw a *U* shape, filling the whole paper. Then draw a line across the top. Add claw feet for the legs of the tub. Outline the tub with a black marker or crayon and then cut it out.

5. Arrange the character and the bathtub on the 12- by 18-inch paper. Place the character partly behind the tub so that it looks like it is in the tub. Glue it onto the paper. If desired, glue a piece of towel or other material to the edge of the bathtub to look like a bath towel.

6. Draw a line for the floor.

7. Cut large circles from the textured bubble paper. Make a pleasing composition by gluing the bubbles around the bathtub. Add smaller bubbles to the picture so that they **overlap** other bubbles.

One Step More

Encourage children to write a story about their character. Invite children to share their stories along with their artwork.

Art Show

Display the artwork on a clothesline, along with children's stories.

 **Bookshelf**

Five Ugly Monsters by Tedd Arnold (Scholastic, 1995)

Green Wilma by Tedd Arnold (Viking Press, 1998)

Huggly's Pizza by Tedd Arnold (Scholastic, 2000)

Huggly Takes a Bath by Tedd Arnold (Scholastic, 1998)

Parts by Tedd Arnold (Penguin Putnam Books for Young Readers, 1997)

New Art Words

horizontal
overlap
vertical
collage

 ## Materials

* 12- by 18-inch colored paper (not blue)
* glue
* blue paper shapes in the following sizes:
  5- by 5-inch squares
  3- by 4-inch rectangles
  3-inch triangles
* black paper shapes in the following sizes:
  2-inch and 3-inch circles
  2-inch squares
* scraps of construction paper in various colors including yellow and brown
* scissors
* white paper cut into 3-inch circles
* markers and pencils
* small pieces of brightly colored yarn
* 9- by 12-inch white construction paper
* examples of patterns found on fabric
* colored paper (optional, for mounting)

The Little Engine That Could

by Watty Piper

illustrated by George and Doris Hauman

Children use simple shapes and colorful patterns to make a paper collage of the little engine and his passenger, the clown.

Let's Begin

Read aloud *The Little Engine That Could* to the class. Have you ever thought you couldn't do something and then, after trying it, discovered you could do it after all? Children may remember learning how to tie their shoes, whistle, zip their own jacket, or ride a bike. How does it feel to succeed? Invite children to share their experiences. What helped them to be successful? The little engine in the story was able to do what some larger engines couldn't, simply because he was willing to try.

Place the precut shapes on a tray or shallow box so that children can easily find and identify the shapes to assemble their collages. Pass out the materials. Then demonstrate the following procedures as children follow along.

Step by Step

1. Place a sheet of 12- by 18-inch paper in a **horizontal** position. To make the large part of the engine, glue a blue square to the center of the colored paper. Then glue a blue rectangle in front of the square so that that it **overlaps** the square slightly.

2. To make the stovepipe found at the front of the engine, find a blue triangle. Glue it in a **vertical** position so that the long point of the triangle overlaps the engine's rectangle.

3. Glue black circles along the bottom edge of the train for the wheels. Glue on the black squares for the train's windows.

4. Cut out a bell from a scrap of yellow paper. Cut out thin brown rectangles to form a rod from which to hang the bell. Glue the rod and bell into place.

5. Observe the illustrations of the clown in the book. Discuss the way clowns apply makeup in different ways to express feelings such as joy or sadness. Select a small white circle for the clown's face. Use a marker to make a colorful nose in the middle of the circle. Use different-colored markers to draw eyes, eyebrows, eyelashes, and a mouth.

 **TIP**

Starting in the middle of the face with the nose may help young children allow the space needed for all facial features.

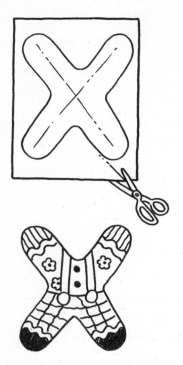

6. Use scrap pieces of colored paper to create a hat made of simple shapes. Glue the hat into place. To add hair, glue small pieces of yarn onto the back of the head.

7. Position a sheet of 9- by 12-inch paper vertically. In pencil, lightly draw a large *X* that fills the paper. Draw a bubble around the *X*. Cut out the shape. This will be the clown's body.

8. Explain that clowns wear many different kinds of clothing. Encourage children to create a colorful costume for their clown. Some suggested clown accessories include bow ties, ruffled collars, buttons in various shapes, belts, and suspenders. Show examples of patterns found in clothing, such as stripes, polka dots, flowers, plaids, and checks. Observe and discuss patterns in clothing children are wearing. Remember that clowns often combine many patterns! Have children draw a colorful, patterned outfit on the *X*-shaped paper.

9. Glue the head onto the body, and then glue the clown onto the 12- by 18-inch paper, overlapping the train. Explain to children that this creates a **collage**.

One Step More

Discuss children's experiences with trains. What noises do trains make? Has anyone ever taken a train ride? Have children think about *The Little Engine That Could* and then write or dictate statements about accomplishing a hard-to-reach goal.

Art Show

Mount the finished projects on larger sheets of colored paper. Attach children's statements about achieving a difficult goal to their collages. Make a paper chain or a track to connect each child's collage.

Bookshelf

All Aboard Trains by Mary Harding (Platt & Munk, 1989)

The Caboose Who Got Loose by Bill Peet (Houghton Mifflin Co., 1971)

Clickety Clack by Rob and Amy Spence (Viking Children's Books, 1999)

The Little Engine That Could by Watty Piper (Platt & Munk, 1990)

Thomas: The Really Useful Engine by Rev. Wilbert V. Awdry and Tommy Stubbs (Random House, 1999)

Trains by Anne Rockwell (Penguin Putnam Books for Young Readers, 1993)